FLUTTER!

Wisdom For Living, Loving, Dying

ED FRIERSON

Art/Illustrations: Mary Jo Perkins
Cover Design: Christopher Darling

ISBN-13: 978-0692287774

Published By
THE BOOKCOMBER
- For Those Seeking Treasure In Books -

Suzan

1957 - 1992

Now, you *know*!

I
MEET CASEY CRAWLEY
compassionate - curious - conscientious

Little Casey Crawley was just four years old when he realized that he knew what the bugs he was observing were going to do before they did it. He would watch an ant scurrying across the sidewalk. When the ant approached a crack, Casey knew that the ant would hesitate, then go to the left just before venturing across the crack. Other ants would first explore to the right. Regardless, Casey always knew, always, which way the ants were going to veer before the ants themselves actually turned!

Casey was just as tuned into beetles, grasshoppers and ladybugs. But, of all the insects, young Casey was most fascinated by lightning bugs and butterflies. He always knew exactly, to the instant, when a lightning bug would flash and which way it would fly next. He could track lightning bugs in the yard on a moonless night and would tell his mother whether a group of the "star bugs" were friends or not. He even told his mother when two of the flying flashlights were talking to one another about getting married.

When it came to butterflies, Casey had an uncanny knack of knowing not only where they would fly next, but also which plant or flower they were looking for.

Though he didn't know the scientific names of the different butterflies, he did learn the names of many different flowers from his mother who loved her garden and her little Casey. She just smiled when Casey pointed and told her that "more orange butterflies will come if you grow more of those." She told Casey that she didn't like the smell of milkweed, the plant to which he had pointed.

At age six, first-grader Casey told his teacher that children were killing many happy bugs in the schoolyard and that the other bugs were confused and didn't know where to go. The teacher replied, "Oh, those are only ants. You don't need to worry about them. We need to keep them out of our school or they will get into the lunch bags."

During recess, while the other children played games, Casey tried to guide the ants away from the school building. Other kids laughed at Casey and began to call him "Bug Boy." Although Casey loved to play games, too, after that he spent most of his free time trying to help insects escape from the certain devastation that would come from other humans who were continually trying to "get rid of the bugs."

By the time Casey was 10 years old, he had become so familiar with the insects in his own yard that he began to give them names. He easily found their nests and gave family names to all of his "friends" as well. More fascinating was the fact that young Casey believed that he could actually understand his insect friends.

"Although they don't talk," he explained, "I still know what they are thinking or, at the very least, what they are going to do."

Casey kept most of this to himself. He had learned that his sympathy for bugs was considered weird. He was embarrassed when his classmates called him Bug Boy. He did everything that he could think of to help bugs and spiders and butterflies live their natural lives, but he also did everything he could think of to be considered a normal boy. Indeed, by the time he was a teenager, no one any longer called him Bug Boy.

When Casey was alone, however, he began to experiment. He knew he was receiving communications from insects and he was determined to learn if he could actually send communications to insects. His first experiments were complete failures. No matter how hard he tried to steer a bug to a specific source of food, or guide a butterfly to a particular blossom, he could not influence what they would do. On the other hand, when he put his mind at rest, he invariably knew what they were about to do.

The young boy, Casey, had discovered an important key. When his own mind was quiet, that is, when he was so beamed in on a specific bug that he had no chatter going on in his head, he would get clear impressions of what the bug was actually experiencing.

When, on the other hand, he tried to communicate to an insect, he couldn't keep the thoughts away. His head would be full of words. Above all, he reasoned, no lady bug, grasshopper, fly or butterfly knew any words.

He wondered over and over what it would take to both receive and send information to his friends, the insects.

Casey began to keep a very private notebook. He started by writing down what the insects were communicating to each other. At first, the notes were mixed up and little more than snippets of ideas that anyone would assume Casey had made up himself.

Then, one afternoon, sitting on the back porch steps, Casey caught a glimpse of a butterfly flitting, seemingly aimlessly, above his mother's flower bed. As soon as he fixed his attention on the butterfly, his mind went quiet, "empty" would be a better word.

An amazing moment occurred. Casey received a full blown impression from the air-dancing butterfly. Later, he would write in his notebook, "It was as close to a human thought as I had ever received."

The butterfly was frustrated! The butterfly was trying to send some kind of message. Casey would subsequently describe his impression as "some kind of inspiration or motivation." The butterfly was apparently "speaking" to a caterpillar that Casey quickly spotted, a caterpillar that was not creeping, just lying perfectly still along a leafless branch in the shrub near the porch.

Astounded, Casey considered his interaction with the butterfly to be so profound and so understandable that he ran quickly to fetch his notebook. It took only half a minute.

The butterfly was still darting about the flower bed when Casey sat down and quieted his mind in the way that he had been practicing. The butterfly was descending among the branches and stems reaching almost to the earth, then rising, then down again, then up and down as if giving a demonstration of butter*flying*.

As he began getting "vibes" from the orange-winged flyer, Casey again had the distinct impression that all the butterfly's maneuvers were directed toward the immobile, almost lifeless, caterpillar on the bare branch. Fascinated, Casey tried not to think any words. Rather, Casey consciously tuned in to both creatures. Immediately, he knew the caterpillar was in a funk. The caterpillar had given up.

As Casey's own thoughts drifted into a faraway mental abyss, he positioned the notebook on his lap and grasped the pen comfortably in a writing grip. Casey descended deeper into the insect world. His head nodded and his eyes closed. Then, his hand began to move. Casey was apparently making notes on a fresh page yet seemed unaware that he was moving.

To an observer, Casey would have appeared to be engaged in "automatic writing," what some might call "trance scribbling," akin to sleep walking. He was behaving in this world at the same time being clearly oblivious to his surroundings and his own actions.

That evening, Casey, the former Bug Boy, discovered that he had been invited into a realm no other human had ever entered. Yet, he could not remember the precise instant of his becoming an insect. Nonetheless, he had been given insect INsights that other humans could some day know. Casey, while his mind was completely quiet and his own thoughts completely nonexistent, had transcribed a "revelation" in his bug notebook.

After reading what he had scribbled while sitting on the back porch, Casey edited his translation. He deliberately omitted the private, personal exchanges between the butterfly and the caterpillar. Casey put a title at the top of a fresh piece of paper.

THE BUTTERFLY REVELATION

Later, Casey added butterfly doodles that he often sketched when especially happy. Though he would continue to doodle, as a young man, Casey began to seriously study the amazing details of each butterfly's wings and, in time, he could accurately draw the indescribable designs, recognizing them for what they were . . . miraculous!

II
THE BUTTERFLY REVELATION
You were born to fly!
MONARCHUS III

translated by

Casey Crawley
Third Millennium AD

May I introduce myself. You may think of me as Monarchus III, one of the distinguished Monarch clan. My grandfather, Monarchus I, was born early this year. He passed on before my father was born, yet he left careful, genetically imbedded instructions for my father to share with me. My father was faithful to the task and, before his recent passing, endowed me with the time eternal *way of transformation* dream. I gave this dream gift to my own son, Monarchus IV, whom you see sprawled listlessly on that nearby leafless branch. He has forsaken the dream. He has stopped eating. He is dying.

Sadly for me, Monarchus IV has given up his preparation for transformation, which, nonetheless, is his birthright. He has succumbed to the common fallacy that his everyday existence leads to nothing worthwhile. Each day, he imagines, will be just like the day before, and the day before that. Monarchus IV has not embraced the truth that *he was born to fly*.

At a recent gathering of "seekers," a caterpillar bunch of which he is a founder, my son concluded publicly, "From a caterpillar egg was I born. As a caterpillar seeking wisdom I have lived. As a caterpillar disenchanted with the meaninglessness of daily creeping, munching, and meandering, I SHALL MUNCH AND MEANDER NO MORE!"

Monarchus IV surmises that he was born of a caterpillar egg. Thus, he limits his understanding of his life journey. He obliterates any view of his own transformation with the leaf devouring blinders of caterpillar routine. Monarchus IV thinks life is futile rather than future-forming. He believes he was born a caterpillar and, based on observations of caterpillar life, will so die.

Thus, with a simple mistaken conclusion, Monarchus IV has shut the joy out of his life. He has lost his faith. He no longer has hope. Although he is being attracted toward a spectacular transformation, tragically, he doesn't accede to it. His faulty conclusion corresponds to the "demise illusion," a viewpoint held by many human men and women. I refer to the birth-to-death notion that many humans accept rather than the birth-to-transcendence sequence that is mirrored in our *way of transformation*.

Mankind has allowed the same kind of misunderstanding to cloud its picture, its understanding of humanity's life journey. Many men and women share Monarchus IV's conclusion that day-to-day eating, striving, building and traveling will all come to a crashing halt at the moment they call "death." These humans have concluded that the meaning of one's life is fleeting. One seemingly wise human leader famously lamented, "All is vanity." Life's accomplishments are ultimately worthless and futile.

I'm afraid that many humans concur with the same fundamentally mistaken conclusion that Monarchus IV articulated. A human might say this: "I was born a human being. I can point to the place and to the time. I can show you the source of all humans, specifically, human ovum fertilized by human sperm. So forget any notion that I was born an *eternal being* on earth.

"I was born in the flesh, with a body to eat, drink, be merry, and fortuitously absorb the traditions and beliefs of others that assuage my hopelessness. I am a human being. I live for a time and I die. I am not a God."

In truth, one does not have to be a God to be an *eternal being*. God is a word to be debated, never to be perfectly understood. The full nature of God is outside of terrestrial man's thinking boundaries. Fret not. Such debating will not affect the odyssey of life at all, just as debating "gravity" does not cause objects to fall upward.

My grandfather passed along a very simple truth to my father. "You were born from a butterfly egg, not from a caterpillar egg."

Imagine that. Our time spent encapsulated in a caterpillar body is temporary. *We are born to fly!* My father instilled this truth in me, genetically embedding it, as had his father before him.

Let us assimilate this certainty. Caterpillars do not *practice* flying. Caterpillars need not even *imagine* flying. Healthy caterpillars live sustained by an inherent urge that leads inevitably to transformation. Though it is their natural heritage to be transformed into light, wispy, magical, flying Monarchs, they simply do not comprehend this truth.

You, human-on-the-porch, are living your caterpillar time. You are NOT a caterpillar person. You are a butterfly person. You are an *eternal soul* born *through* a human egg and human sperm. That is, you are a *spiritual being* whose characteristic immortal quality pervades every cell of your body, just as the butterfly blueprint is found in every cell of a caterpillar body.

You do not *practice* celestial living. You do not need to *imagine* celestial living. Rather, you ought to live serenely as a terrestrial being embracing the thought that you will undergo a remodeling. In the twinkling of an eye, you will be transfigured into a "light being," an eternal, wispy, magical energy cluster, which is your natural heritage. Such a notion may feel strange to you, yet you are drawn to it.

I experienced a comparable feeling as a creeper that I have come to fully appreciate only since becoming a flyer. Being descended from butterflies, each caterpillar is endowed with an obscure yearning. The yearning might best be understood as an urge to be a self-fulfilled member of the butterfly community, though such a community is, in fact, unknowable to the caterpillar. Thus, any depiction of butterflying and its nature are beyond the understanding of even the most advanced, deeply pondering caterpillar. I did not have an urge to fly, just to cocoon.

The inherent caterpillar urge toward an unknowable, unimaginable realm of flying creatures has an even more mysterious complement. As opposed to the "pushing" of a built-in impulse, the complementary urge acts as a magnet, "pulling" each caterpillar. It is as if the life giving element of all creation continuously exerts a pulse-wave signal beckoning the awareness of every living thing to realize the oneness, the singularity, of all life. The originator of the pulse-waves of attraction which caress each caterpillar, is continuously integrating into itself the "life" within all creatures.

Butterflies call this root of all living by the word "Flutter." Where there is Flutter, there is life. You, human-on-the-porch, will no doubt read, discuss and wonder about this life source.

Humans use words such as "spirit," "vibration," or even "Word." A well known expression says, "In the beginning was the 'Word' . . ."

Our understanding is that Flutter is within, as well as through and about, each caterpillar, each branch, each leaf, each breath. It is impossible to exist and be separated from Flutter. Flutter is the underlying mode as well as the material of all creation.

We can experience Flutter in an almost infinite number of ways, but the *essence* of Flutter is a single, unfathomable ALL-THAT-IS. One ancient scribble that I enjoy even though I do not fully understand it says that "Flutter is God breathing."

I do, however, understand the implication of an essence that includes ALL-THAT-IS. We are interconnected. Flutter touches all simultaneously. Just as your eye sees where your feet are landing and your ear hears what a distant clock is chiming, Flutter sees, hears, feels, indeed, breathes every living creature's breath. Flutter guides us even as you direct your eyes and ears.

Flutter does not insist, it allows. You are free to come as close to or stay as far away from anything or anyone as you choose. Flutter simply registers your choices and the recordings are maintained, forever available, should you care to reflect upon them.

By the way, I did not find you by mistake, nor did Monarchus IV randomly choose to give up his life struggle in your mother's garden. Your affection for insects, bugs, beetles, fireflies, butterflies, ants, caterpillars and grasshoppers was whispered throughout our world. Unknown to you, by your affinity for all creation, you drew us to yourself. You chose us!

Before I go on my way, I want to clarify what I have found here concerning my son. Monarchus IV became sidetracked. As a thriving, young caterpillar, Monarchus IV, acted upon the momentous truth, *You were born to fly*, that was embedded in his heart. He had embraced the satisfactions and discouragements of daily routine, with faith, and joy, and hope. Then, unfortunately, he abandoned the *way of transformation* because he saw only futility in the lives and demise of his companion caterpillars. He couldn't "see" the future. He squandered his faith.

With all my heart and soul, I focused directly on the living essence within the near lifeless body of my promising son, Monarchus IV. He responded feebly, but reasonably. Weakly, Monarchus IV restated his position, "I see nothing worthwhile ahead. Why continue a purposeless caterpillar life?"

Upon my insistence, Monarchus IV considered that while he is surely free to discard what he has not witnessed, he is just as certainly free to believe, and to act upon, that which he has not witnessed. I implored specifically, "Monarchus IV, YOU were born of a *butterfly egg*. Your natural heritage is to live the *butterfly life!*"

Monarchus IV has decided to believe he was born of a butterfly egg. His point-of-viewing has begun to shift. He is becoming a new caterpillar, accepting the revelation on faith, choosing to trust its possibility. You will find him once again chomping toward his cocoon time with this admittedly unwitnessed truth propelling him . . . consciously. You see, futility, which is a matter of perspective, can dissolve when one observes life from a new point-of-viewing.

As a flyer, I see now what Monarchus IV has yet to see. I remember when I, too, had a creeper's point-of-viewing. Talk of flying was considered to be gibberish by many of my closest friends. Oh, if they could see me now. They would concede that *You were born to fly* was the simple truth all along.

Our ancient airborne Monarch wise ones determined to share with their creeping caterpillar descendants many truths discovered from a flying point-of-viewing. Beyond that, for posterity, they set out to record other discerned truths inexplicably embedded *within* their nature. The complete collection of these truths, or "INsights," is known as *The Butterfly Revelation*. *The Butterfly Revelation* heralds this unveiled timeless wisdom in the form of perishable scrawls smeared by snail collaborators on often overlooked leaves. Every caterpillar generation discovers some of these wisdom revealing leaves.

In this garden there is a caterpillar seekers bunch who daily contemplate scrawls they have found on leaves bearing written fragments of *The Butterfly Revelation*. I am certain that Monarchus IV will rejoin the group when his physical strength returns.

I recommend that you check in on Monarchus IV when your curiosity about the lost-and-found INsights of *The Butterfly Revelation* has reached an unquenchable moment when you yourself long to know more about our timeless truths. It is believed that the full *Revelation* applies equally to all living creatures, including humans.

I think you will find that *The Butterfly Revelation* INsights speak wisdom to human yearning during the human caterpillar stage in much the same way as they have spoken to each generation of our Monarch clan. Perhaps you can be instrumental in preserving and communicating this special wisdom to other humans who feel intuitively that much more is known about life, death and the hereafter than is commonly shared.

Now, to you, human-on-the-porch, I say "Goodbye." And, as I said to Monarchus IV, "Happy munching . . . and, savor, really savor, each bite!" I, Monarchus III, shall savor these moments with you.

Casey was mesmerized, dumbfounded by his own notes. His life was about to change. Of that he was certain. He determined to find Monarchus IV and the caterpillar seekers who were mentioned. Frankly, he had no idea what would happen. He did not even notice that at this moment he himself had become a bonafide "seeker." That he, Casey, possessed the gift of revealing was not yet known.

On this momentous day, when Casey learned of the so-called "butterfly wisdom," heretofore unimagined by him, Casey wrote in bold block marker letters on the cover of his notebook:

THE BUTTERFLY REVELATION

Casey Crawley

A dozen years passed. Sitting on the porch steps with the ever expanding notebook on his lap became a ritual for the lad.

As Casey grew older, he began to read the biographical writings of men and women whose spiritual seeking had resulted in their having unusual experiences. He was drawn to written accounts of especially insightful humans, those known as Holy Men and Holy Women. He began to keep a diary-of-ideas containing the thoughts of such rare individuals. He found that none had ever engaged another species, much less insects, as a source of revelation.

III
THE GIFT OF REVEALING
An INsight Out Treasure

Is communicating with bugs and butterflies a delusion . . . or a miracle? Is connecting with insect wisdom outrageous . . . or enlightening? Is Casey Crawley's notebook itself a fairy tale . . . or a revelation? Does Casey have the gift of blarney . . . or the gift of revealing? Whatever your inclination at this moment, you would be wise to set it aside . . . or, at the very least, be prepared to recalibrate. You just can't make this stuff up!

One surprising summer day, Casey, who was now a young man, experienced a dèja vu moment. Sitting on the steps of his mother's porch, Casey was rereading the transcript he had trance-scribbled in his notebook many years earlier. He began mentally to relive his boyhood encounter with Monarchus III, the butterfly, and Monarchus IV, the caterpillar. Some would say that he was "lucid dreaming." Others might think, "time warp." Whatever.

Inexplicably, as if it had happened just yesterday, Casey began to experience, to relive his first, years-ago, encounter with a butterfly. Unexpectedly, a very real, very bright orange butterfly flippity-flapped through the air directly in front of Casey's half closed eyes. The butterfly landed on the very branch which, on that many years ago *yesterday*, had supported the forlorn caterpillar whose name, Monarchus IV, Casey had found in his sleep-written notes.

Casey was now wide awake! However, he was brain shocked. He was so startled by the nearby presence of the orange butterfly that his mind went blank. He locked on to the butterfly as though, for the moment, nothing else in the world existed.

Time stood still. Then, as he would journal later, Casey's mind shouted silently within him, "MONARCHUS?!?"

Give this next notebook entry a chance. Deliberately, withhold your pre-judgment. Let Casey share his experience as he lived it.

"In my mind's ear, I heard the butterfly's voice answer," Casey wrote. "Either I am totally delusional, delirious and cuckoo, or I have just experienced an episode of INsight, intuition and interconnectedness beyond anything I might have imagined."

For someone today reading all of Casey's notes, this first reported encounter with the mind and soul of a living insect provides an introductory glimpse into a wondrous resource, *The Butterfly Revelation*, which it would be Casey's lifelong grand endeavor to unveil. Casey's true gift, extremely rare and richly rewarding, is the gift of revealing. The capability to reveal what is within the mind, heart and soul of another of any species is, indeed, a precious *INsight Out* attribute.

According to Casey's notebook, "I received a simple response that sounded to my inner ear as if it might have been spoken by a self-confident stranger who I was meeting for the first time. I responded by merely thinking what I would say.

"Of course, I did not actually know how to speak to butterflies in an insect language. Strangely, in my interconnected state of mind, it didn't seem to matter."

"Yes. My name is Monarchus III, a proud member of the distinguished Monarch Clan. May I have the honor to know your given name? Your reputation as a friend of insects is well known."

Casey: "My name is Casey."

Monarchus III: "Ah, Kay-SEE', a name that you must cherish. You have INsight, which is the ability to 'see' within another. It is an extraordinary characteristic, somewhat rare I might add. I predict that you will become a very special 'see-er,' one who can reveal INsights drawn from our insect world to curious individuals in your human world."

CASEY: "I am not at all sure what to make of your presence. I see you balancing mutely on the branch, yet I hear you distinctly. And, honestly, I am dumbfounded that I understand you. Somehow I am in your head and you are in mine. Is this what you mean by INsight?"

Monarchus III: "That explanation is as clear as it is possible to express."

Casey: "Before you fly away, there are some things I would like to ask you."

Monarchus III: "I shall be happy to stay for awhile. Then, I want to check up on my son who, you remember, was on this very spot *yesterday*."

Casey: "Oh, indeed, I do remember. And, what happened *yesterday* is what I want to ask you about.

"Apparently, while my conscious mind was disengaged, my subconscious mind led me to record everything you wanted me to know about your son. I also found that you had mentioned a mysterious source of wisdom, *The Butterfly Revelation*, that contains truths for all species. I shall not be happy until my curiosity about this wisdom is quenched, if that is possible."

Monarchus III: "That depends entirely upon you. Curiosity seems to be a trait that can be satisfied easily in some and seems nearly unquenchable in others. Only you yourself can decide when your wisdom threshold has been reached."

Casey: "Well, I want to know everything about *The Butterfly Revelation*. What can you share?"

Monarchus III: "Only what I myself have experienced. After all, that is the only true knowledge that anyone can ever share. We can *know about* countless subjects, but, beyond what we experience, in reality, we truly *know* nothing. Now, where would you like to begin?"

Casey: "I am not sure where to begin. I do not have a clue what questions to ask. I guess I want to know the what, when, where, who, how, and why of *The Butterfly Revelation*. Ha. There are six questions that I learned to think about when making reports at school. Begin with them, if you please."

Monarchus III: "This is not school. The best I can do is to share a bit of what I ***know***. It may not be as simple as you would like it to be. While there is obvious wisdom in *The Butterfly Revelation*, there is considerable mystery.

"*The Butterfly Revelation* is thought to have originated among our earliest ancestors and it is said that modifications are made by deeply thoughtful butterflyers of each generation. There is even speculation that some *Revelation* ideas come from minds that no longer have bodies, but I am highly skeptical of such a notion."

Casey: "I am a skeptic by nature, so I would be quite satisfied to learn about only that which you *know* to be authentic."

Monarchus III: "All right. I will begin with a fascinating *Revelation* secret. Such little known ideas are preserved as 'scrawls' written on leaves where wandering caterpillars may discover them. This particular secret was carefully inscribed on a slender leaf, slithered by an artistic snail who was a special friend of my grandfather. The same scrawl was also found on several fragments from even earlier generations. Indeed, the complete collection of our ancestors' wisdom scrawls is known to us as *The Butterfly Revelation*."

Casey: "Oh, how I would like to learn of all the secrets. Is this possible?"

Monarchus III: "My advice? Find my son. The current caterpillar generation seekers' group, of which Monarchus IV is a co-founder, repeatedly studies newly discovered scrawls at its regular gatherings.

"For now, I will share what I believe is one of the grandest, most exhilarating INsights ever revealed. Such ancient sagacity speaks of a time of great wisdom, a wisdom that has nearly been lost.

Eternity Is Now. They are one and the same!

"This notable *Butterfly Revelation* INsight expresses an idea that many human beings have struggled mightily to communicate after experiencing 'enlightenment,' or what we might call, their 'butterfly futures,' or their 'celestial homes.' Words alone cannot convey such experiences. Words help us *know about* this kind of experience, not truly **know** the experience itself.

"However, the words speak a hidden truth. Every moment of existence is 'now.' There are no other moments. Whatever was, is, or shall be always exists ONLY in the 'now' that is happening. 'Forever' and 'now' are interchangeable. Anything that is 'forever' is happening 'now.' What do you think?"

Casey: " I hardly think at all. For me, this is merely a new way to express familiar words. I am curious, however, to know why you are so exhilarated by such a simple sentence."

Monarchus III: "You want to know why this truth ought to buoy the heart and mind of all living creatures? Consider what I shared *yesterday* about the root of all living, what we call Flutter. I said, 'Flutter always was, is, and always shall be.' Thus, at this moment, all that *ever* was living, moving and being within the domain of Flutter, is not only living 'now,' but also synonymously, is living 'in eternity.' We are eternal beings!"

Casey: "Is there any evidence to support such a fantastic statement?"

Monarchus III: "According to your human investigators, your theoretical scientists, 'Matter, is neither created nor destroyed. It only changes form.' Humans speak of these changes as transformations. In butterfly lingo, these changes are called 'flutterations.' All transformations, that is, flutterations, occur within, never outside, the domain of Flutter."

Casey: "Oooooh, I see why you consider this a secret. I had never heard this conclusion."

Monarchus III: "As for this secret and my feelings, I am about to burst with expectation, for soon I will experience another redesign. I will abandon butterflying and embrace another stunning cosmic flutteration which is simply unimaginable to me in this moment.

"You see, I have been privileged to share my earth life experience and my earthly *way of transformation* perspective with you here and now. Yet, in just a short while, I must forego the earth vibration to which I am accustomed. I am to undergo another incomprehensible change. I can hardly wait to experience what I am to become."

Casey: "You are going to become something different? You are not going to be a butterfly? Forgive me if I offend you, but are you not going to simply die? Butterflies do die, you know."

Monarchus III: "I would have thought that, too. However, *The Butterfly Revelation* offers another way of thinking about life and death. The here and hereafter may not be what they seem to be.

"Find my son and his friends. Learn for yourself the wisdom of our ancestors and decide for yourself what to embrace and what to discard."

Casey: "Wait, you expect me to believe that you are not going to die?"

Monarchus III: "No one can give his or her innermost beliefs to another. What ideas to accept or reject is a matter of individual choice. What you *experience*, on the other hand, is 'truth' for yourself, which no one can either give you or take away from you. Your experience, your personal truth, is yours and yours alone. Your experience creates your beliefs. My experience creates my beliefs. You and I are free to believe what we will."

Casey: "But you said you expect to become something else rather than to die. What experience has led you to believe that?"

Monarchus III: "Encountering *The Butterfly Revelation*. The INsights from the ancient wise ones became my very own. How it happened is still a bit of a mystery to me. I cannot explain it. Find my son! Experience the wisdom of *The Butterfly Revelation* for yourself."

Casey: "Would you be kind enough to offer me some truth that you learned from experiencing the scrawls first as a caterpillar creeper and, subsequently, from experiencing life as a butterfly?"

Monarchus III: "Certainly. I was completely baffled by the scrawl, *You were born to fly*. My life experience revealed its truth."

Casey: "Ah, a weird idea from your caterpillar perspective became a simple matter-of-fact when your transformation was complete. The scrawl was not speculation nor prophecy. It was truth that you had not yet experienced. Is that a fair statement?"

Monarchus III: "Quite fair. Before I leave you, let me share a bit more INsight about the *Eternity Is Now* scrawl. I think it will begin to open your mind to the power of *The Butterfly Revelation*. I trust my interpretation will arouse an even greater curiosity about life both here and hereafter as revealed in the *Revelation,* what we often call our 'INsight Out' treasure."

Casey: "I could hardly be more curious."

Monarchus III: "In a single moment, a 'now' that will come to pass, I will inherit from my true source, a nature that is unfathomable to me at this moment of 'now.' How do I know this to be the truth? I have already had a comparable experience! Remember, as a caterpillar, a flying life was unfathomable to me.

"Consider. The *butterfly* eggs from which Monarchus I, Monarchus II, I, myself, and Monarchus IV were born, all were infused with Flutter. Every cell of my being has been and still is Flutter-full. When these wings no longer flap, and this body no longer flits about, my Flutter containing the true 'I' will rejoin the great fabric of the 'Flutter-That-Is-ALL.'

"What I will become in that flutteration moment of 'now,' I simply cannot comprehend in this moment of 'now.' No matter. I could not comprehend flying before I began flying. Flying? Flying is simply glorious! What is to come? Beyond glorious, I feel certain.

"What you call 'dying,' my destined remaking, according to *The Butterfly Revelation*, will be a 'now' moment, and it will be 'eternal.' They are one and the same, interchangeable. I, majestically, will change in form and in substance incomprehensibly different from that which my earlier flutteration from caterpillar to butterfly produced. Whatever lies beyond flying must be resplendent!"

Casey: "How can this idea have any meaning for me and my human friends?

Monarchus III: "I cannot interpret for you, of course. Personally, I have a strong inclination to accept that a 'now' makeover moment is the same for all species, including man.

"For mankind, a moment of seemingly miraculous transformation will occur. At one moment of 'now,' a human being is integrated into a terrestrial body. At the very next moment of 'now,' that same human being is fully functioning within a celestial energy form. In neither moment is the human being, terrestrial or celestial, *ever* separated from, nor outside of, the source of all life, 'God breathing.' Understand this, human-on-the-porch. Whether, for the moment, someone's abode is terrestrial or celestial, each someone lives . . . NOW."

26

Casey: "That you, a butterfly, have this depth of thought completely 'blows me away,' as we humans say. You seem to be drawing on a universal source of information, not an insect memory bank. Is there anything more that the *Eternity Is Now* scrawl reveals?"

Monarchus III: "Properly understood, the *Eternity Is Now* scrawl asserts that moving from terrestrial to celestial existence marks only a startling moment of 'now.' Other *Revelation* scrawls clarify that this sublime moment is a moment which affects the *vibration* of a life, even a human life. A *higher vibration* allows one to exit the restraints of a terrestrial body including its limitations and pains.

"In contrast with terrestrial vibration, celestial vibration is not confined nor defined by a certain space. Celestial existence is a totally different experiencing of 'now,' as different as a butterfly experiences its airborne life relative to its very own surface bound caterpillar life before cocooning.

"Chrysalis . . . dark . . . unknowing . . . imprisoned . . . silent . . . void like. Then, BINGO! Light! One moment, the cocoon; the next moment, experimenting with a whole new life style in an extraordinary new 'life jacket.'

"For you, human-on-the-porch, at some single moment you will *be* as a 'terrestrial soul.' The very next moment, you will have *become* a 'celestial soul.' We all are *being and becoming* at each moment in time."

With that, the radiant orange butterfly flew straight up, seeming to bow two or three times, before streaking away . . . never again to be seen in the garden that Casey now loved more than ever.

Casey wondered to himself, "Am I dreaming? Is that what is happening? No. No way I'm dreaming. Just look at these notes."

Musing, "I feel as if I have been involved in a high flying seminar, well, a seminar with a high flyer, I suppose I could say. Who would believe this? Nobody! Anyone would think I was making it all up."

Casey determined that he would keep a truly complete notebook. In addition to his regular insect *observations*, he decided to include any new insect *interactions* should they occur. Casey never dreamed that what would eventually fill his notebook was more startling, more revealing than any of his nighttime dreams. For anyone who has ever wondered, "What happens when you die?" *The Butterfly Revelation*, Casey's own name for his notebook, was to become an incomparable source of wisdom.

Casey discovered that he did, indeed, possess INsight, an ability to get inside, to actually **know**, what an insect was experiencing. Unknown to himself, through his careful note keeping, Casey was perfecting his special gift of revealing. Casey would reveal to the world a kind of wisdom that had never before been known. Casey's Bug Book would become an *INsight Out* treasure as foretold to him this day in his mother's garden . . . by a butterfly!

For Casey, his answer to the "What happens when you die?" question, and the revealing, began when he wrote of his experience after finding a rejuvenated caterpillar, Monarchus IV, and his friends.

Casey dubbed the INsight seeking group, The Caterpillar Club. The Caterpillar Club as revealed in Casey's notebook is next.

IV
THE CATERPILLAR CLUB
Buckeye Jr., Janice, Lawrence, Melissa,
Monarchus IV, Pixie, Vanessa, Woolly Bear

- Casey's Notebook -

For several years I have been receiving detailed impressions of the communication existing among insects of all kinds. Joyously, for me, when I am able to shut off all my own thoughts, my mind translates everything I receive into fully understandable human language. To those who may someday be curious about the caterpillar seekers and their desire to understand *The Butterfly Revelation*, I begin by reviewing what I know.

As a young boy sitting on the porch, I connected to a spectacular orange butterfly who was desperate to arouse a completely lethargic caterpillar lying hopelessly still on a bare branch nearby. The butterfly, Monarchus III, disclosed to me that the listless caterpillar was one of his sons.

Further, the desperate butterfly, Monarchus III, revealed that his Monarchus clan is privy to an ancient wisdom. He explained that the *way of transformation* wisdom has descended through countless generations by means of genetic embedding. Astonishingly, I learned there is also another means of wisdom transmission, a physical means. Oily smearings on the surfaces of leaves can and do convey messages.

Sadly, only fragments of such scrawls are ever discovered. The INsights obtained, therefore, are often sketchy and puzzling to the finders.

Alongside a well-worn insect path, near a caterpillar meeting circle, several scrawls of butterfly wisdom had been deposited. They were smeared on the undersides of some overhanging leaves. These wise scribbles were the work, actually excretions, of a talented, but lugubrious snail who had been enlisted for the task by none other than Monarchus I, the outspoken leader of the first generation of Monarchs to emerge in this location.

The message fragments are assumed to be excerpts from some sort of far distant past collective family treasure. The treasure needs to be rediscovered in each generation and deposited anew for the next generation. Admittedly, it is a hit-and-miss proposition for each new group of seekers. The *way of transformation* science is akin to building a house without the full architectural drawings, and with some of the bricks missing.

The caterpillar club story begins with the discovery of some *Revelation* fragments by Monarchus I's great grandson, Monarchus IV. This caterpillar, Monarchus IV, subsequently became profoundly disillusioned with the process of seeking, which earlier, upon discovering the fragments, he had exuberantly embraced. In fact, he preferred to quit eating rather than to continue the "non-sense of staying alive," as he put it.

Using significant reminders from the *Revelation* itself, Monarchus III, his butterfly dad, helped his caterpillar offspring to reverse course and resume his chomp-chomp life.

Waking from a dream state, it may have been *yesterday* or *yesteryear*, I found that the grand orange butterfly was urging me to connect with his son's caterpillar seekers' group. I was captivated by his butterfly promise. His promise? He said that I would discover that the *way of transformation* and *The Butterfly Revelation* wisdom INsights have counterparts in human society.

Indeed, I did discover the group of caterpillars that Monarchus III called "seekers." Happily, I do understand them! I know now, in fact, that I have been given the gift of revealing, the ability to translate INsights emerging from a different point-of-viewing, a Monarchus Point-Of-Viewing. Nothing more important has ever happened to me!

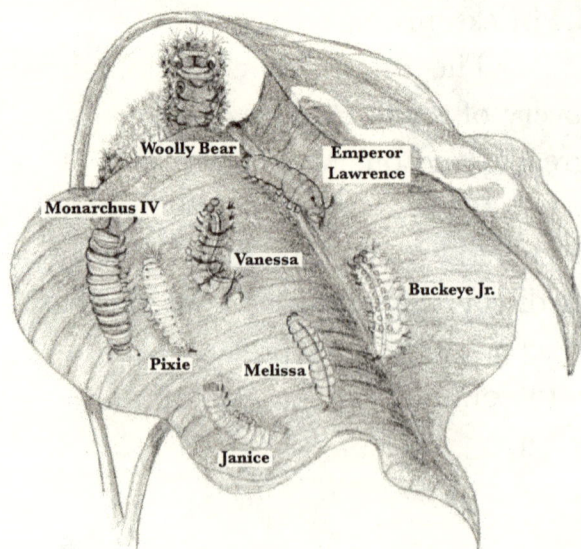

I have come to know each caterpillar seeker quite well. They remind me of my human friends and acquaintances. (I'll name no names. You may recognize yourself, however.)

The caterpillar gatherers prefer to call themselves "seekers," not members, since it is not a group one must join. It is a group that every caterpillar is born into, yet many do not know this. "There is not a single prerequisite for seeking," according to the shaggy Woolly Bear. "Once you even *think* a question, any question, you are a seeker."

These notes are something of a sketchy journal detailing my observations of and impressions emanating from each of the seekers. For me, the most compelling notes I am making are those which illuminate for humans the wisdom of the caterpillar forerunners, which, as it turns out, were not caterpillars at all. The wisdom is that of *The Butterfly Revelation!*

So that I might share what I am learning in a practical way, I have given each seeker a common human name rather than use the sophisticated scientific name that he or she bears. Naturally, the caterpillars themselves are not aware that they even have names. As hinted in the *Revelation*, using names (i.e., language and labels) often interferes with pure **knowing**. Pure **knowing** includes, both for caterpillars and humans, **knowing** who and what you truly are.

—∿—

33

Monarchus IV

Monarchus IV was not a visionary caterpillar. Though charming, Monarchus IV rarely thought about anything other than the leaf he was chomping at the moment. It would be fair to say that, early on, Monarchus IV was quite pedestrian in outlook, thoroughly lacking inspiration and slowly becoming disenchanted with the monotonous munch-and-meander way of life into which he had been born.

Monarchus IV had inherited his great grandfather's charisma, yet, at times, he relapsed into a brooding, lethargic, self pitying forager. Ironically, it was while in the company of another thoroughly discouraged crawler, a lovely caterpillar named Pixie, that he spotted the first of a *Butterfly Revelation* scrawls cache.

The nearly intact INsight collection found by Monarchus IV also contained many obscure symbols. Curious, Monarchus IV contacted the much admired caterpillar, Woolly Bear, who was known to be really smart. Woolly and Monarchus IV together deciphered most of the scrawl fragments.

It was Pixie who sweet talked Monarchus IV and Woolly Bear into helping found the club that was to be "devoted to the discovery, discernment, and dissemination of our ancestors' wisdom." Woolly, Pixie and the newly enthusiastic Monarchus IV spread the word that everyone was welcome to join them daily to seek and discern, if possible, the scrawls' deeper meanings.

Five caterpillars responded to the invitation. To the greater population, wisdom seeking is considered a frivolous distraction from the real work of living. To most, living means eating, period. At times, other curious creepers did come to the gatherings often returning for a few sessions before dropping out. Lamentably, some early gatherers, and even one founder, had tragically shortened lives.

Monarchus IV, to be sure, was intrigued by what he had found. Discovering the first scrawl had aroused his latent curiosity. He did not realize that Pixie's suggestion to start a study group was merely a calculated thought that she hoped would allow her to be near Monarchus IV on a regular basis. She was beguiled by his charisma. She hadn't learned of his muddled mind, his hidden disappointment, and his pessimistic outlook.

Fortunately for Pixie, Monarchus IV's curiosity overcame his growing disenchantment with his mundane life. Voila! The Caterpillar Club was born. The name is my invention. The group is known by another name to the caterpillars themselves.

—⁓—

Shortly after the discovery of the first INsight scrawl, the eight caterpillars, each from a different family tree, began the daily gatherings. Initially, the newly energized Monarchus IV led the discussion and used his affable style to ensure that all expressed themselves without a hint of reprisal, embarrassment, or feigned agreement.

The club had no preconceptions whatsoever. No idea was suppressed. No formality was enforced. There were no members. Each gatherer was self directed and, fittingly, soon referred to himself or herself simply as a seeker. After all, the group was *looking for something*. Oddly, from the perspective of outsiders, no one could define just what it was that the group hoped to find.

The gatherers had questions about life. They were seeking answers that might be hidden in everyday sight. Ah, the scrawls! They hoped that in the newly discovered INsights from an earlier, and perhaps wiser time, they would find those answers.

The seekers especially liked one of the first messages to be deciphered. *You cannot BE different than you are right now . . . you can BECOME different.* Unanimously, from that day forward, they decided to call themselves, "The Being & Becoming Bunch."

Though they call their group The Being & Becoming Bunch, everyone else just calls the gathering, The Babblers Bunch, or The Blabbers Bunch. I can't determine which exactly.

36

Dismissively, within their own community, these earnest self-improvement caterpillars are unsympathetically called either Babblers or Blabbers by the other caterpillars.

The Caterpillar Club meets every day under an umbrella of shady hosta leaves in the middle of mom's beautiful flower garden. My mother calls the plants "plantain lilies." The caterpillars' spirits are light-hearted, but their discussions are serious. They have different personalities. Shortly, I will tell you about each of them.

An especially poignant idea was offered at the second gathering. "I think we would all like to find significance for ourselves," said Buckeye Jr., who was the quietest, most reflective member of the group. There was an immediate murmured acknowledgement. At once the mumbling agreement was interrupted. "Yeah, what are we doing here?" two others blurted almost simultaneously.

Responding, Lawrence, a self-proclaimed "Emperor," an uninhibited, somewhat blatant caterpillar, declared loudly, "We KNOW what we are doing here. We are eating leaves! Don't we mean, 'What's the point of it all?' 'How come we are alive?' Am I right?"

"I think also," said Monarchus IV smoothly, "that we would all like to know what is ahead for us. What will our future be like? What will we become?" Those truly WERE everyone's questions.

Buckeye Jr., the quiet one, added, "INsight #1 may be a 'truth,' but it leaves us all hanging." He was referring to the enigmatic statement,

"Eternity IS Now. They are one and the same."

This is a deep secret INsight according to Monarchus III, whose perspective I have included elsewhere. "I hope we will be able to figure out what it means," Buckeye said seriously.

Another seeker, Vanessa, who had not yet spoken, then interjected a provocative topic followed by a truly nebulous question. "I hope to someday make my cocoon. What happens then?"

The other gatherers were immediately enveloped with an eerie silence. No one EVER talked openly about the cocoon. Assuredly, the subject was on everyone's mind each time a family member disappeared into the husk that he or she had so diligently created.

The consensus among caterpillars was that anything beyond the cocoon was unknowable. Unknowable, that is, unless something known by the ancestors, the ancient seers of an earlier generation, had actually been revealed and was now hidden.

Indeed, above all other questions and answers, the seekers wanted to find the answer to the BIG question, "What happens *after* the cocoon?"

Woolly Bear glanced around the group. "Each of us is curious. Each of us has expressed a yearning to know more about where the every day effort to live is actually leading. We all wonder if munching around is all there is. As seekers, we hope the ancient wisdom fragments will answer a very personal question." Woolly paused for effect. "Am I all that I will ever be?"

Woolly has a knack for summarizing. Suppose we learn more about him.

"Woolly Bear"

The group, which I have named The Caterpillar Club, is now led in its discussions by the sober and sophisticated caterpillar named Arctiidae, whom I call "Woolly Bear." Woolly is a splendid caterpillar both in appearance and demeanor. Woolly has always been popular with the other caterpillars.

While many are strikingly more colorful in appearance and more agile in their exaggerated inch-walking, Woolly is totally fuzzy, fluffy, what some call "adorable."

Throughout the grind of formal caterpillar education, Woolly was cooperative and genial, never shy, yet never intrusive. Teachers and students alike were very fond of Woolly. And, Woolly was smart in a natural kind of way, not just a book smart smush head. He liked to look at all sides of an argument and never felt the need to "one up" others with his own conclusions.

During his brief caterpillar schooling, Woolly's ability to compare and contrast was rewarded with high marks. Now, as a mature discussion leader, never does he fail to take a comment, even the most banal observation, and treat it to contextual and exegetical analysis.

Each day, before the serious discussion begins, Woolly leads the group in a brief chant. The chant is clearly an archetype idea from *The Butterfly Revelation* which undergirds most everything the club members seek to understand. All intoning together, the sound chorus is extraordinarily harmonious.

"I be. You be. We be.
A.T.? We *shall* be!"
("A. T." I understand to mean "After Transition.")

Today, rather unexpectedly, one of the seekers asked, "Is there a clear way to explain our daily affirmation?"

For some time, I, too, have pondered the meaning of the chant. I understand that the chant is, indeed, an affirmation.

We humans, too, express affirmations, or our beliefs, in our rituals. I was delighted when Woolly summarized the convoluted discussion that followed.

Woolly suggested that each participant substitute the word "live" for the more nebulous "be." The ritual couplet now says, "I live. You live. We live. After transition? We *shall* live!" But what is meant by "transition?" I'm befuddled. The gatherers seem satisfied.

After that clarifying discussion, the opening ritual has now been tagged with an epithet. The seekers now refer to the refrain as their "Life Chant."

As before, every meeting of The Caterpillar Club begins with the members' rhythmic reaffirmation. There is a mood creating and mind focusing quality to the gatherers' melodious incantation. Woolly says that, while it is a living, or "being" chant, it is also a "becoming" chant. He calls it a "Destiny Chant." I have dubbed some of his contributions, "Woollyisms."

Woolly's personal analyses of recovered *Revelation* fragments seem profound. Yet, at each meeting he injects pithy phrases, "Woollyisms," that are not of *Butterfly Revelation* origin. To club members, his glib utterances are considered gems of wisdom and are repeated as aphorisms, maxims and mottos whenever someone asks what club members learn. That other caterpillars, the non-seekers, find such platitudes to be tedious and esoteric clap-trap does not deter members from collecting these axioms and plastering them everywhere.

It is a problem now along the most popular trails. Ancient wisdom INsights are interspersed among attention-grabbing slogans. Admittedly, sometimes it is difficult to tell the difference. The confusing clutter of vacillating jargon among timeless belief statements is being created by the very ones who are seeking clarity. What an irony! I see the same thing among human beings.

One iconic wisdom-slogan INsight was on a leaf recently pruned away by my mother. It said,

"Don't wait for eternity. Eternity is NOW."

41

"What baloney," said a non-seeker crawling past. "No one wants to live like this *forever!*" There was even talk of forming a group to systematically rub out the scattered "wis-dumb scrawls" as they were derisively called.

Even the great prophecy declaration, *You were born to fly,* with its hopeful promise of a different life, is vehemently ridiculed. Non-seekers often snidely redirect the implied message toward seekers as they work together on a leaf that is being group-chomped.

"Go ahead. Jump! You can fly, right?" The non-seekers then break into a great group caterpillar wiggle, the equivalent of human jokesters cracking up with laughter.

Woolly sometimes is caught up in his own discussion prowess. When there are grainy differences of opinion, he has begun not to assuage, but to pontificate. I think Woolly is becoming emotionally trapped in his own eminence.

When meeting time is over, the other seekers get right back to the seeming endless tedium of chomping leaves with their families. Woolly, however, does not return immediately to his family.

Rather than getting on with his preparation for cocooning, Woolly often lollygags under the Hosta leaves and mutters to no one in particular. In fact, there is no one to hear him! He loves to invent erudite sounding jargon that is catchy and easy to memorize. Regretfully, the phrases are mostly shallow and insignificant, merely witticisms, unlike the meaningful *Butterfly Revelation* INsights.

Woolly Bear, the promising intellectual, is becoming his own audience. Sad. He is no wiser for having encountered *The Butterfly Revelation.* He is satisfying himself with his own cleverness.

Extra! Extra! The analysis above is no longer true.
Woolly Bear, while struggling to unravel
the wisdom scrawls, sloughed off
his unattractive conceit and
regained his dignity.
- Details later -

Melissa

The most peaceful member of The Caterpillar Club is Melissa Lycaeides. Melissa is a friendly companion who is "at home" wherever she travels and with whomever she spends time. She is the essence of enjoyment. Curious and careful, persistent and playful, imaginative and sincere, Melissa is widely admired for her blend of energy and tranquility. Above all, Melissa embodies a patience born of optimism. She believes the future is sure to be bright.

Melissa is convinced that she will discover all she needs to discover. She feels sure that she will learn all she needs to learn. She is certain that she will be able to do all she needs to do to carry out her life's role. She has the sense that she is honestly moving forward to fulfill her place and purpose within all creation itself. To others, Melissa is a part time Pollyanna because she insists that every day is glorious, though not always beautiful.

When pressed to explain her unflagging enthusiasm for an often monotonous daily routine, Melissa occasionally reveals her "faith." She repeats, "Today, we may unravel the mysteries of the *Revelation*; if not today, one day soon." One thing never changes. Melissa is cheerful.

"Emperor" Lawrence

Lawrence is continually searching for greener leaves which, to him, always seem to be on the other side of the street. The self aggrandizing "Emperor" often flouts his risk taking, seeing himself as all-brave while he views the other club members as all-talk. Lawrence quite often disregards potential risks. His modus operandi is to "do whatever it takes" in pursuit of quality meals. To Lawrence, the I'll-do-as-I-please style represents courage.

"Sometimes it is the high risk price you pay that gives you the greatest pleasure," Lawrence explained during a club discussion about what a satisfied life should be like. He loves to call attention to his willingness to crawl cross the street just to sample the leaves on the other side. He brags that the heat of the asphalt would never deter him from the great pleasure of sampling certain delicate buds "way beyond two curbs" that the others would never taste.

Lawrence loves to flaunt his devil-may-care attitude. Unfortunately for Lawrence, while he dared to challenge the roadway heat, he had no way of learning about the effects of oversized, steel radial tires.

From The Emperor's perspective there was no such thing as "squish." He had never even heard of the word. Often, in remembrance of Lawrence, members of The Caterpillar Club would remind each other, "What you don't know CAN hurt you!"

Needless to say, the heat of the street surface was nothing compared with the weight of an SUV tire. And, know about it or not, "squish" perfectly described the final moment of The Emperor.

Buckeye Jr.

Buckeye, Jr. was downright envious of certain worms. You might say he coveted their high flying style. What he observed was that, after every rain, the lowliest worms were given free sky rides by the robins. The robins had sturdy legs, sculpted beaks, robust bodies, and amazing wings. Ahh, to be sure, the robins were objects of awe and wonderment among all caterpillar club gatherers.

During and after a rain, most caterpillars remain hidden and secluded under the leaf canopies in the garden. Buckeye Jr., however, could not control his overwhelming desire to "play worm" and hitch a ride beyond all comprehension--a ride to the sky!

"The rest," as they say, "is history." An alert robin spotted the plump Buckeye Jr., and, indeed, gave him the ride of his life. Watching Buckeye Jr. disappear into the sky was one caterpillar club memory that took on a mythical storyline of its own.

The "Flight Of The Buckeye" became the subject of caterpillar legend. The spot where the ascending caterpillar left the earth was commemorated with a marker. A hymn was written honoring the memory of Buckeye Jr.'s last days on earth. "Plucked by a robin" was seen as a grand alternative to the cocoon . . . and dying! "Buckeye Jr. will never die," says the legend.

Some caterpillars, including at least two caterpillar club gatherers, speculate that Buckeye Jr. has been taken to another, more glorious garden. It is told with great conviction that Buckeye Jr. will forever live in this lush garden somewhere beyond the blue called "Heaven."

Other caterpillars even imagine that where "Jr." has been taken he will no longer be driven to cocoon. He will no longer chomp his days away. He will be snatched regularly, just for fun, into the sky for a ride. Legend lovers commonly remark that Buckeye Jr. has "gone to heaven."

Heaven, that indescribable atmospheric garden, is imagined to be located at a place somewhere only the robins know for sure. The robins, then, are perceived to be messengers from Paradise, the Garden In The Sky.

Frustratingly, though the birds chirp incessantly, caterpillars know the robins will not tell where they have their sky haven. And, in fact, when pressed, the robins absolutely refuse to talk about Buckeye Jr. except to say that "of course, we know where he is."

The Caterpillar Club gatherers determined to settle, once and for all, what it meant to be "plucked by a robin."

While they agreed that to be plucked was an honor, the seekers disagreed as to what Buckeye Jr. had done to deserve such an honor. Briefly, they set aside their study of the ancient wisdom scrolls in order to analyze every activity and interaction that was known to involve Buckeye Jr. The goal was to create a code of conduct for all caterpillars to follow that would be based on Buckeye Jr.'s life.

"After all," some seekers reasoned, "we all want to live forever. Believing in the Buckeye Path and following it seems the surest way to achieve immortality."

Actually, no one truly believes it! Most say that there was only one Buckeye Jr. "To live *like* him and not *be* him would be a sham." Buckeye Guidelines were developed . . . and ignored!

Vanessa

Vanessa was exuberant and exhilarated by each caterpillar gathering. However, after a few days, the enthusiasm ran out. Vanessa's pursuit of wisdom intoxication caused her to be the most obnoxious blabber, and annoying babbler, of all the seekers. She "turned off" everyone who was not inclined to inquire about the *Revelation* fragments that had been deciphered. As she turned others off, Vanessa was shunned by them. For a gregarious caterpillar, that was devastating.

Vanessa had enlightenment to sell. Indeed, she longed to give it away.

After each daily gathering, Vanessa literally disgorged her overflowing, newly ingested "INsights" by babbling away to every caterpillar within range.

Trouble was, the neighborhood caterpillars were all chomping toward their cocoon time and were disgusted that Vanessa was blabbing rather than eating. In her everyday world, Vanessa was thought to be an "air head."

Younger caterpillars were taught to look away and avoid contact with Vanessa. Older caterpillars were always "too busy" to listen. They had enough to do without hearing again and again about the wondrous revelations uncovered by the caterpillar "kooks" during The Being & Becoming Bunch discussion sessions.

In time, Vanessa decided to give up on her "lost" family and acquaintances. She began to look in other environments for prospective companions and converts.

Unfortunately, while traveling away from her familiar community, Vanessa came upon a shimmering web with its interlaced, symmetrical, step-ladder-trails. It seemed like an exciting, and admittedly glamorous, place to begin her crusade.

Schluck, schluuuck, schluuuuuuck. Vanessa was startled and scared. The shimmering steps that she had eased onto were mucilaginous, sticky, gluelike. Vanessa was trapped. Her last sensation was that of being wrapped strand by strand by nonstop strand with a substance that she could not comprehend.

Vanessa had wandered into a land of spun webs and deceits. Glitter had become glue. Her message would never be shared. Her enlightenment in the form of ancient adages had succumbed to the world of eat-or-be-eaten. Vanessa would never know that she, too, had possessed the capacity to spin a web of her own, a cocoon.

Had she continued on the *way of transformation*, Vanessa would have spun a *web of life*. Her desire to gain converts to an incomplete caterpillar understanding had prevented her from becoming the airborne, sky traveler with a butterfly nature which was her natural destiny. Vanessa succumbed in a glittering *web of death*.

Janice

The saddest gatherer was Janice, who was also the most devout. She embraced an odd message of hope, "Someday, I'll climb over the rainbow." She attended every single gathering, and kept a complete file of the "Profound Points" which were derived from the *Revelation*.

Janice independently established an exercise calendar to which she slavishly devoted herself never allowing the normal activities of community life to intrude. Janice rarely smiled. Janice rarely spoke. For her "faithfulness and dedication," Janice was honored at a special reception.

In time, Janice was pretty much left out not only of the routine pleasures of the neighborhood, but also the grand events, the celebrations and the hoopla which marked the collective joy of being alive with those who shared her space.

Janice became totally devoted to discovering the mysteries of the rainbows whose colorful spectacles she had experienced when peering just beyond the garden, over a nearby curb. One purpose of her diligent exercising was to gain strength enough to go over the curb one day in search of the wonders that she knew must lie at the end of each rainbow. She obsessed over her conviction that on the other side of the rainbow was a land where cocooning was not needed.

Janice found that the other seekers were not as fascinated by rainbows as she was. They agreed pleasantly that rainbows were, indeed, special. However, none of the seekers ever believed that an end-of-the-rainbow-treasure existed. As for the Land Of No Cocooning, the gatherers told Janice that should she ever find such a place, "be sure to come back and tell us."

Chasing her rainbow obsession, Janice hurriedly left a club gathering as a passing thunderstorm was subsiding. "Today," she thought, "I will make it over the curb and beyond the rainbow."

While focusing on the prismatic arch, Janice lost her balance and slid headlong into a maelstrom of water swirling curbside. The rushing stream created by the thunderstorm swept her the length of the street and she was washed down into the sewer near the corner.

Although Janice was not missed within the larger community of caterpillars, her absence was significant at the next Being & Becoming Bunch gathering. Her disappearance engendered an aura of mystery.

There was an animated discussion hinging on the question, What will she become when she reaches the end of the rainbow? "Do you suppose," Woolly invited the others, "that there is any truth in her strong belief that there is a Land Of No Cocooning?"

There was sustained silence until Lawrence announced, "Well I for one am NOT going to follow her to find out." Coming from the ultra adventuresome Emperor, on that note the discussion ended.

"We do have one new matter of business," announced Woolly. "Who will volunteer to keep the file of the Profound Points that Janice kept," and, in a rather pompous after thought, Woolly added, "to which I regularly contribute?"

Pixie sidled over to see what Janice had gathered and saw that Janice actually had two lists! One was titled "Profound Points." The other list was clearly titled "Pontificated Points." Each entry on that list had the initial "W" beside it.

Pixie instantly knew that the Pontificated Points were not from the *Butterfly Revelation* scrawls, but rather, were some of the clever quips that Woolly had made up. "Right on, Janice," she thought to herself. From that time on, Pixie sometimes thought of their venerated discussion facilitator as "Woolly The Puff," though she would not dream of saying it to his face!

Pixie

Pixie is that special character who learns all the right things even if, seemingly, for the wrong reasons. More than any other seeker, Pixie is following the *way of transformation* with joy, humor, excitement, tranquility, purpose, and satisfaction. She "gets it."

Pixie loves seeking. She loves companionship. She loves wrestling with *The Butterfly Revelation* scrawls. She loves waking every day.

Pixie endures the rigors of endless dawn-to-dusk leaf chomping with grace and dignity. She comforts non-seeking neighbors with undisguised affection. She admits that she knows "nothing at all" about what she is becoming.

Pixie revels in "just being what I am . . . at least for the moment." Above all else, SHE ADORES MONARCHUS IV.

"From the first time I laid eyes on him," Pixie confided to her closest friends, "I knew we would live our lives together in a special way. I decided to do every thing I could to be near him."

Pixie once told her love story to a non-seeker. "I had no idea that *The Butterfly Revelation* even existed, much less what it was. When Monarchus IV found the first fragments, I knew right then and there, the enigmatic *Revelation* was one of the ways to his heart. At the time, I didn't know any other way. I'm not sure, even today, that I have entered his heart. It doesn't matter, though. Because of the *Revelation*, I get to be near him, and that is good enough . . . for now."

Pixie took over the arduous task of maintaining the collection of age-old INsights that were analyzed at each seekers' gathering. In fact, because of Pixie's love for Monarchus IV, she has become as determined a seeker as he.

Clearly, Pixie did not start out to be a vessel of ancient *Revelation* wisdom. She met the perplexing scrawls with no curiosity at all. She just loved being with Monarchus IV.

To some, it seems as if the wrong reason led to the right learning for Pixie. I don't think that. I think there is no such thing as "the wrong reason." There are only reasons. We judge a reason to be right or wrong with the benefit of hindsight. Using foresight, a reason is often merely an idea leading to an action that one hopes will work out for the good. We win some and we lose some.

Hopefully the winning outcomes, those where we seem to have acted for the right reasons, occur as much or more than the not-so-good outcomes. Good luck with that!

It is a high probability guess that Pixie is the one caterpillar from this group who, after transition, will be inspired to place her eggs, imbedded with the most illuminating wisdom, in a carefully chosen location. And further, it is highly probable, that she will find a way to coax a snail or two into smearing the precious wisdom nuggets on to strategically placed leaves that may be discovered by the next generation . . . perhaps by two caterpillars in love.

V

THE REVELATION "SCRAWLS"

and

The Spirit Of The Blue Dazzler

documented by

Casey Crawley

Third Millennium AD

During each caterpillar club gathering, the caterpillars struggle to understand at least one scrawl, a wisdom fragment, smeared on the surface of a leaf. The caterpillar seekers like to say, "the truth is hidden in plain sight." They approach the scrawls with the same single mindedness that daily they give to their mundane munch-a-bunch survival existence. I admire the caterpillars' determined effort to unravel the tantalizing "truth morsels" they have discovered.

The source of these ancient truths is referred to as *The Butterfly Revelation.* The *Revelation* itself is comprised of a mysterious collection of ideas that transformed caterpillars have attained. The chasm between what a caterpillar and a transformed caterpillar (butterfly!) can experience is uncrossable; yet, every new generation of caterpillars produces extraordinarily sensitive individuals who are driven to unravel the secret teaching of each fragment that is found.

Three timeless *Revelation* INsights have already been entered in this notebook. They were communicated to me by Monarchus III, the first ever butterfly with whom I connected.

Often referred to simply as "the scrawls" by the caterpillar seekers, the first three INsights I received were:

(1) *You were born to fly.*

(2) *You cannot BE different than you are . . .*
you can BECOME different.

(3) *Eternity Is Now . . .*
They are one and the same.

On occasion, I have discussed similar ideas with human friends who, quite sincerely, believe they, too, have discovered hints of an ancient wisdom that have been lost. Usually, these big ideas are not truly lost, but rather are drowned out by the hustle-bustle found in crowded human enclaves that sometimes number 25 million or more in a single city.

When not concentrating on *The Butterfly Revelation*, the caterpillars often analyze their every day lives seeking to make sense of their existence. Often I am startled by the caterpillars' ideas. Their conversations seem intermittently as profound, yet similarly puzzling, as many human discussions in which I have participated.

Recent examples of what I call "caterpillar thought gems" I have grouped here. I think these sparkling ideas reveal a parallel between the caterpillars' urge to live a quality life and our human resolve to accomplish "a life well lived."

Happiness is . . . sharing a leaf.

Fun is . . . laughing at creation's whimsy.

Joy is . . . basking in the light of a sunbeam.

Peace is . . . a shady spot on a sweltering day.

Kindness is . . . a gentle nudge upward on a
difficult branch.

Satisfaction is . . . knowing you are almost
ready to cocoon.

Community is . . . a group squirm
going nowhere.

These thought gems are pleasant enough and I wrote them down because we humans often write books, poems, songs, and plays which offer a wide range of similar action definitions. However, we humans have elevated three grand ideas to a status somewhat above that of the qualities just listed. In a letter to Corinth, a biblical writer summarized, "these three remain: faith, hope and love, but the greatest of these is love." (I Corinthians 13:13)

My caterpillar friends have considered the same qualities and, when I am immersed in their consciousness, their impressions and my admittedly limited human language somehow coincide. The understandings are theirs, the words are mine.

Faith is . . . imagining what might be,
   without fear.

Hope is . . . the notion that there must be a
   grand creative mind that knows
   what's up at all times.

Love is . . . a soul-heart pulsating in harmony
   with one or more other soul-hearts,
   and all resonating in sync with the
   very heartbeat of God.

The Butterfly Revelation fragments reveal even deeper truths not only about love, but also about life, death, and the mystery-after-death. Profound! There is no other word to characterize what I am about to share.

I have located a comfortable shady spot overlooking the caterpillar gathering place where I am able to sit resting against a tree trunk which is slanted just to my liking. From my "observatory" I am able to tune in completely to the actions, thoughts and feelings of the caterpillar gatherers.

Believe me, I know what you are thinking, "nothing like this has ever been reported before." Trust me. I'll share exactly what I experienced. And, you are right. Nothing like this has ever been recorded.

Today, The Caterpillar Club is considering a somewhat puzzling fragment. The message contains a surprising subject and an imperative suggesting an action to be undertaken. Just three words are being pondered. A lively discussion is taking place. I am fascinated by the three words.

Behold The Raindrop

To the caterpillars, raindrops are mysterious. They drop from the sky. They bubble up on leaves and in puddles on the ground. They are absorbed by plants, splashed about by the birds, and deliciously ingested by all the insect families. Then, as the sun beams down, the remaining raindrops simply disappear.

The caterpillar seekers are at a loss to explain the importance of the scrawl. "After all," said one seeker, "we want to know how we got here, what we are doing here, and what happens after we cocoon."

Another gatherer concurred, "Raindrops enable us to survive, but they provide no INsight into our greatest questions."

The discussion takes off. "Raindrops fall from nowhere," mumbles a confused seeker. "What's to behold, the splash?"

"No, not so," says a convincing seeker. "Raindrops fall from heaven."

"Well," a quizzical third seeker chimes in, "How did the raindrops get to heaven in the first place?"

A thoughtful, deliberate seeker adds, "I think in heaven the raindrops are created out of nothing. Once they are ready, you know, kinda full, they just naturally come down."

The convincing voice adds a somewhat deeper thought. "If raindrops didn't come down, we would all die. The grass, the bushes, the trees, the leaves, EVERYTHING would die. No raindrops, no life! That's the way I see it. *Behold The Raindrop* has something to do with life itself."

At this point, the discussion leader eases in, "Just a minute here. Don't raindrops themselves die? I mean, one morning they are everywhere, and after the sun comes out awhile, all the raindrops die. They disappear. They cannot even keep themselves alive."

After a significant silence, a usually quiet seeker affirms, "That's true. That's very true."

A fresh, new voice gets the group's attention. "When I behold raindrops, I think of how delicious a rain soaked leaf can taste. That's it. That's all I think when I think about raindrops. I don't see any connection between raindrops and cocooning. I and a raindrop do what we do. And then, we both disappear. End of story."

The leader looks carefully at each seeker's face. "Are we agreed? This thought, *Behold The Raindrop*, is a dead end. Raindrops have nothing to teach us." Each face seems satisfied. "Well then," suggests the leader, "Let's go on to the next fragment."

A slightly nervous seeker shifts everyone's gears, "Hadn't we all better get back to our respective families' munchfests? Everyone except us is laboring today, all day long."

Every caterpillar in the circle is wobble-nodding what seems to be a gesture of agreement.

The nervous seeker continues, "Perhaps it would be best if we agreed not to mention today's subject. Remember, the last time raindrops came we were all flooded. Many of our friends were washed away in the gullies that were created by raindrop torrents. I think our families are afraid of raindrops even if they do bring life. I know I am afraid when I hear thunder."

"Double agree," said the leader, "Let's forget today."

After a long, uncomfortable silence, the leader confidently offers, "Tomorrow's scrawl could be the one we are hoping for, one that answers our questions. Let us not be discouraged."

The caterpillars begin to inch away as if their minds and hopes have been set adrift. Several do seem discouraged. The raindrop scrawl clearly has stymied The Caterpillar Club.

I, too, feel adrift in my own pondering. Why *Behold The Raindrop*? What is the significance of such an instruction? Is this wisdom? I simply don't get it. My thoughts are drifting away . . . away . . . away. My mind is empty.

Without warning, my mind, my consciousness, is invaded with a "presence." I know no other word to describe the moment. I have no thought. I am not dreaming. I hear no voice. I simply have the distinct impression, I **know**, that I have tuned into another living consciousness. I am simultaneously experiencing myself *and* another. I am not groggy or passive. I am highly energized. My body is relaxed but I AM ALIVE IN SPIRIT!

I have my notebook on my lap. I have a gel pen in my hand. I am beginning to **know** my "visitor."

This is an experience unlike any that I have had heretofore with a bug, an insect, a caterpillar, or a butterfly. I see nothing or no one. I am completely melded with an unseen life. Two living spirits are one, at least for the moment.

My eyes are closed. My breathing is deep and rhythmic. I begin writing. The two spirits begin "speaking" to each other as clearly as I speak with my friends every day. My own silent "voice," inside my mind, conveys my curiosity, "What or who are you?" I am using words-without-words! Incredible!

I pick up a response as if I were in a conversation with an interesting new acquaintance. The response is real.

Such mind exchanges I now describe as *"**direct knowing**."* Here is what is coming through . . . clear as a bell.

The Other: "I was always known as 'Blue.' To be perfectly honest, I was the most beautiful blue butterfly to ever air dance above the earth. I am not bragging. The simple truth is that our family was given our distinct beauty by the creator. Why and how anyone speaks such a truth can be a problem, of course. By speaking the truth about the dazzling beauty of my family, I honor the creator of all beauty. My beauty certainly was not my own doing."

Me: "Do you have a name? Have I met any of your family?"

The Other: "We are the Peleides, thank you. Had I been asked, I would have chosen a lovelier name, a 'nickname' you would call it. Suppose you write that when I was a living butterfly, I would have loved to have been called 'Idyllica.'"

Me: "Why?"

The Other: I was known as the 'happy and peaceful one.' That's why I would have used the name, 'Idyllica,' had I been in charge of naming. Please, feel free to think of me as idyllic. And yes, you have occasionally seen some of my descendants."

―⁓―

The spirit of a Peleides! In my mind! Crazy?!? No, real! Before I could think a word of response, Idyllica, the butterfly spirit, *knew* what I was going to say!

Idyllica, the butterfly spirit, did not need my words. Idyllica, the butterfly spirit, was experiencing ME. Whatever words I might have chosen, the butterfly spirit completely **knew** them as soon as I did. Incomprehensible . . . for the time being.

I realize now that using the exact words, or language of any kind, is superfluous to **knowing**. Language interferes with the **direct knowing** of another being. Language is very helpful for *knowing about* another being. However, for truly **knowing** another, language is unnecessary.

I, at this moment, **know** Idyllica in spirit. For each other, we do not need words. For you who may read this notebook, I will continue to use the very best words I can think of so that you can *know about* my time united with Idyllica.

I want you to understand what I am learning from Idyllica and from *The Butterfly Revelation*. Given the difference between **knowing** and *knowing about,* I hope *knowing about* my experiences may inspire you to seek a **knowing** relationship, spirit with spirit, for yourself.

Me: "Idyllica. That is a lovely name. I, myself, would have loved to have been known as 'Casey The Idyllic.'

"I was known as 'Bug Boy' and was sometimes ashamed that I truly loved bugs. I often felt sad and angry when other kids created havoc for my bug friends.

"No more! I am not sure that anyone would ever understand, but since discovering The Caterpillar Club, I feel very happy, connected, idyllic, to be sure. Idyllica, I think we may be kindred spirits."

Idyllica: "Yes, I know. That is why I have chosen to resonate with you for a brief time. I think that together you and I might help great numbers of humans become happier and more peaceful. Would you like to work toward that goal?"

Me: "Oh, yes. I just need to know how to do that."

Idyllica: To begin with, you have the perfect name. Your name, Casey, means 'brave' in some parts of the world. Your name in English was actually derived from a Polish word which means 'Proclamation Of Peace.' Together, our names, Idyllica and Casey, suggest happiness, bravery, and a double dose of peace."

Casey: "I'd be proud to be your partner for peace. Is that what you mean?"

Idyllica: "Actually, together we may help individual seekers find true peace *of mind*. Everyone who learns more about life, death, transformation and transcendence finds new vigor, happiness and joy for daily living, and feels great comfort and peace **knowing** what to expect when the limitations of the earth vibration are no longer in effect. *The Butterfly Revelation* INsights are the keys to such joy and peace, you know."

Casey: "How can *The Butterfly Revelation* be the key? I am confused by the fragments that have been discovered by Monarchus IV. The caterpillar seekers are struggling mightily, yet unsuccessfully, to understand them. I am afraid our capacity to interpret the meaning of *The Butterfly Revelation* is quite limited. Perhaps the meaning cannot be discerned and will be forever unknown."

Idyllica: "I, my friend, am familiar with many of the first INsights that were ever agreed upon. I do **know** what they mean. I devised many of them. At the elders' urging, I wrote them!"

Casey: "You wrote them?!?"

Idyllica: "Sort of . . ."

Casey: "Sort of?"

Idyllica: "I did, indeed, create several of the key wisdom reflections; however, to be precise, writing down the ideas using snail-slime-scrawling required cooperation which was not easy to obtain. Snails can be stubborn and quite demanding, especially when bartering for their most precious resource. Within a few generations, I am happy to report, we butterflies had developed a workable symbiosis with the snail-scrawlers and the INsights have survived though some of them have, unfortunately, become indecipherable."

Casey: "You actually **know** the meaning, the secrets, of the scrawled thought bundles that The Caterpillar Club seekers are trying to unravel?"

Idyllica: "Oh, yes. The 'beacons,' as they were sometimes called, are much less mysterious than you imagine them to be. The dilemma is not the complexity of the light-giving statements."

Casey: "What *is* the problem?"

Idyllica: "For caterpillars, fully understanding the INsights, or beacons, requires a transformed consciousness. Transformation, or flutteration, occurs only during cocooning for caterpillars."

Casey: "Cocooning. Hmmm, that is the process we humans know as metamorphosis. We know that healthy caterpillars encase themselves in a cocoon and emerge as butterflies."

Idyllica: "Yes. However, from the caterpillar perspective, the cocoon seems the end of life. Before cocooning, even the most ardent caterpillar seeker will always be hobbled by the limitation of earthbound experience. No caterpillar can *know* anything other than that to which he or she is firmly stuck. A caterpillar cannot even imagine flying!

"Some seekers, such as those with whom you are communicating, yearn to *know about* the seemingly unknowable mystery beyond the cocoon. What they learn will always seem to them to be foggy."

Casey: "I suppose the same fog applies to humans."

Idyllica: "No, not at all. The human consciousness can embrace not only its earth-home vibration, the entire terrestrial experience, but also, under very attainable circumstances, the human consciousness can experience celestial existence *as you and I are now experiencing*! The only fog which limits human understanding of the light-giving beacons is, at any given moment, related strictly to the extent that one's mind is cluttered."

Casey: "Cluttered?"

Idyllica: "Yes, a mind occupied with *terrestrial vibrations* is essentially cluttered. Everything that the human body perceives and processes engages the mind. The conscious mind is fully occupied with earthly matters when a human is seeing, listening, touching, eating, and so on. That attention to every day living relegates most *celestial vibrations* to the limitless capacity of the subconscious mind. When a human learns to quiet the clamoring conscious mind, the spirit soars, and the expanded mind may be guided throughout the entire celestial realm, the expanse of all creation."

Casey: "I'm lost."

Idyllica: "Well, let's get specific. That ought help you find yourself."

Casey: "Good, I need you to be specific."

Idyllica: Would you like to **know** the full rich meaning of the advice, *Behold The Raindrop*? It is one of the beacons that I myself wrote."

Casey: "YES! But what if I don't understand?"

Idyllica: "For the moment, we are one-with-each-other. Our consciousness, our combined individual thoughts, are joined. By our sharing a single, intrasoul vibration, you will understand what I understand. As one human scripture writer indicated, in a spiritual union 'we **know** as we are **known**.'"

Casey: "True enough. I am, indeed, resonating with your perspective regarding *Behold The Raindrop*. I just want to choose the best words to share what I am learning with all the future readers of my *Butterfly Revelation* notebook. How do I do THAT?"

Idyllica: "Oh, indeed, feel free to share. For my part, I will help by encapsulating my understanding in human language. I will talk the talk, not just walk the walk. Any curious reader of your notebook will get exactly what he or she is ready to receive. Now, are you ready?"

Casey: "Again, thanks. Yes, indeed, I am ready."

Idyllica: "A raindrop is simply one 'plop' of what you call 'ocean.' All the raindrops, falling all the time, falling everywhere on earth, would, at any moment, change the ocean NOT at all! Every plop comes from the ocean and returns to the ocean. Do you follow that notion?"

Casey: "I'm on board. Thanks for translating your unique understanding into everyday language."

Idyllica: "We recognize that raindrops may also manifest as steam, ice, and clouds. These plop clusters of ocean are all normal."

Casey: "Am I to imagine that the oceans of the earth could be boiled, frozen, and floated skyward?"

Idyllica: "No imagination required. Upon reflection, humans know that a raindrop may have many appearances. That is to say, knowing that a raindrop is 'water' does not do justice to the raindrop. A raindrop is both an individual spheroid of water and, at the same time, a traveling plop-of-ocean, which will, sooner or later, experience the immobility of frozen crystallization, and the gravitational tug of falling from a floating cloud."

Casey: "I haven't thought of a raindrop as being a plop-of-ocean. That is a new point-of-view for me."

Idyllica: "There is an additional twist. In a baffling disappearing action, raindrops regularly vanish into thin air! Any ocean plop, unexpectedly swirling into the upward draft of searing volcanic air, or sitting in a pot boiling over a fire, may torridly evaporate into gas. Such a moment is seemingly the end of a particular raindrop. It is not the end of the ocean."

Casey: "Breathtaking. The 'Journey Of The Plop' would make quite a story."

Idyllica: "The journey of *every* plop makes quite a story."

Casey: "Ooohhh, I am excited by what I am about to learn, and how you are going to say it."

Idyllica: "Let us *Behold The Raindrop* at this point. Let us put ourselves in the plop's shoes for minute. Let us experience as a plop experiences. This changes our point-of-viewing."

Casey: "Ah, yes. My point-of-view is how I think about something. My point-of-viewing is where I am, or imagine myself to be, while thinking about something. So, I need to think of what the raindrop might be experiencing rather than what I am experiencing as a raindrop watcher. Plop on!"

Idyllica: "A plop that finds itself in the soil soon brings life to a seed. A plop that gurgles in the well at a desert oasis helps sustain the wellbeing of a thirsty camel. A plop that travels through a thorny bush eventually triggers the bloom of a rose. A plop that dribbles from an eave into a rain barrel is enlisted to swab the stable floor.

"A plop that is snagged by a star spangled, red and white striped banner hanging from a skyscraper pole majestically waves as patriots salute. A plop that creeps from the mouth of an aged patriarch falls on to a pillow as the worn out body draws its final breath. A plop that trickles across an infant's face glistens as the babe struggles at the breast to learn the fine art of sucking and swallowing.

"A plop gets compressed between two mouths whose lips seem determined to never part. A plop sprays off the metal hide of a monster engine whose launching could bring destruction to untold numbers of unsuspecting earth dwellers. A plop squirts quickly through a hollow needle and brings healing to a body in distress and hope to millions so stricken. A plop is wind blown above a white capped mountain and magically bursts into a delicate hexagonal snow flower. A plop clings to a glass windshield as a relentless rubber wiper slaps it back and forth, back and forth, back and forth . . ."

Casey: "Whoa, every plop lives a different story. To what end is one thing I wonder."

Idyllica: "The end depends upon the story. A plop may be commandeered to save lives or to destroy them. A plop may be induced to create beauty or to spawn ugliness. A plop, when separated from its source, is on its own, bearing unimaginable qualities for good or for naught. When plops are joined together, the resulting composite has an immense potential for construction or destruction on a scale of almost unlimited magnitude."

Casey: "I sense the same might be said about individual human beings."

Idyllica: "Perhaps. Perhaps not."

Casey: "Perhaps not?"

Idyllica: "Simply said. A plop is a plop is a plop. The source and destiny of all plops is the ocean. The INsight beacon simply reads, *Behold The Plop*! No mention yet of humans."

Casey: "I am with you. I sense that you are choosing these words very carefully."

Idyllica: "Yes, I am speaking most deliberately now for readers of your notebook."

Casey: "And, for ME!"

Idyllica: "Your *individual mind* is a 'plop.' YOU are a raindrop. Behold!"

Casey: "Our minds may be likened to raindrops?"

Idyllica: "Water is the basis of life on the earth. Mind is the basis of *awareness* of life.

"Without water there is no living body, no *dwelling*. Without mind there is no consciousness, no *dweller*. This is the non-secret of the scrawl which, unwisely, the gatherers discarded."

Casey: "I am afraid that I, too, dismissed the scrawl's message as irrelevant. Now I wonder, is there more to be understood when contemplating this particular *Revelation* advice?"

Idyllica: "First, the most useful approach is to limit linguistic reasoning, that is 'word matching,' and to increase the 'play of consciousness' itself. Let your mind wrap itself entirely around the word *picture*, rather than arguing away at the words alone.

"Many highly intelligent seekers continually strive to interpret each element of a simple word picture hoping to find a perfect fit or, contrarily, to find some flaw in the picture thus demonstrating its inadequacy. Such efforts limit real INsight."

Casey: "I think I am very much inclined toward a specific interpretation, toward 'word matching,' as you call it. For example, I want the ocean to be the repository of All-The-Mind-That-Is. That lets me think of each person as possessing an actual replica of that which makes up the Mind-Of-God, for example. Then, as I keep reasoning, I begin to have a logical way to explain how the very 'spirit of God' might be embedded in every living organism, especially every human being."

Idyllica: "That's fine. Reasoning and analysis are thinking tools. They can lead toward the treasure. However, there comes a time when the seeker leaves these tools behind. The treasure itself, God realization, lies beyond reason and, according to some skeptics, is completely *un*reasonable, thus non-existent."

Casey: "Well, I like to reason. I can't help but notice that just as some raindrops may be very visible, others are completely obscure. Yet, all raindrops have life giving potentials. "Similarly, I would reason, perhaps every person has God indwelling whether that presence is visible or obscure to others. Oh . . . and it occurs to me that just as life sustaining water in our bodies may be unnoticed by us, God's presence may be hidden from our mind's awareness . . . aha! . . . overwhelmed by the CLUTTER!"

Idyllica: "You are quick to grasp implications. Your mental tools of reason and analysis serve you well. You are going to love *The Butterfly Revelation!*"

Casey: "Without your choosing to resonate with me, I'm afraid I'll be as hopelessly lost as my Caterpillar Club friends."

Idyllica: "I will happily remain within your mind as you and your caterpillar friends focus upon additional scrawls."

Casey: "Before we get together tomorrow, I have a question. Have I received a full understanding of the declaration, *Behold The Raindrop?*"

Idyllica: "No. Your own human teachers have penetrated this idea to an even deeper level."

Casey: "Really? I would welcome an example of this deeper understanding."

Idyllica: "One eloquent human teacher used the word picture, 'Father,' to represent the consciousness of all creation."

Casey: "That would be Jesus of Nazareth."

Idyllica: "Yes. Others use the descriptive word, 'source,' or the more definitive word, 'origin,' when referring to the idea of a 'Creator.' Jesus offered a deeper INsight when he is quoted as saying, 'I and the Father are one.' That is to say, 'My self consciousness is the same as the sustaining consciousness of all that is known to exist.' That thought has great depth."

Casey: "In what way is this statement a so-called deeper INsight?"

Idyllica: "That such a straightforward assertion can be so clouded by misinterpretation suggests that many seekers are shallow-minded.

"Such seekers will argue the linguistic, cultural and cognitive merits of such a statement. These are surface matters, a part of the rational clutter that blocks an individual from experiencing an idea more deeply."

Casey: "Please, guide me deeper."

Idyllica: "Of course, gladly. Jesus did not say, 'my body is synonymous with God.' He said, 'If you see *me*, you see the Father.' He might have just as easily said, 'I and the Father are created from the same stuff.' It is a bit like the cliché, 'If you've seen one, you've seen them all.' O.K. with that?"

Casey: "And how does that square with the raindrop clue, I must ask?"

Idyllica: "Jesus's explanation is similar to my saying, 'If you see a raindrop, you are seeing the ocean.' One is a portion of all that is the other, and is identical to it in nature."

Casey: "So, consciousness, or what many call 'spirit,' is the same whether you engage that spirit in a single person or experience a moment of enlightenment during which moment you **know** you are one with the spirit of all creation. Am I reasoning correctly?"

Idyllica: "Yes, and those expansive moments are what sages consider to be moments of 'complete surrender' of the flesh to the spirit. For those individuals who continuously worship, or are in awe of this holy union, the experience is real.

"In addition to using the term, 'Father,' the best phrase describing the union experience is simply, 'the presence of the Holy Spirit.'"

Casey: "Holy Spirit?"

Idyllica: "Yes. Using the phrase, 'Holy Spirit,' is similar to my describing one aspect of the ocean as 'rain cloud,' or 'cascading waterfall,' or 'bubbling brook.' Another eloquent spokesman, the poet David of Israel, used the word picture, 'He leads me beside the still waters, He restores my soul,' to describe his consciousness completely enraptured with God's peace, God's Holy Spirit, God's presence."

Casey: "These folks are thousands of years removed. What about now?"

Idyllica: "You may say the same things they said. After all, their minds are within you."

Casey: "Help me with that idea."

Idyllica: "You may rightly say, 'I (my conscious awareness) and the Father (the consciousness of all life) consist of the same stuff.'"

Casey: "This is a huge idea. I *know* you are spirit. I now realize that my self-consciousness is also spirit. A simple leap-of-faith allows that I, too, may say, 'I and the Father are One.' Is this right?"

Idyllica: "You have grasped the scrawl's deep truth. Yet, there is something more."

Casey: "Even more? To me, this is the ultimate idea. Are we going beyond reason now?"

Idyllica: "Not yet. Let's take a small, *reasonable*, thought-step further. Contemplating *Behold The Raindrop* opens the mind and heart to the Love of God, to LOVE's eternal presence.

"An open mind and heart grasps this truth: you and I are expressions of the Holy Spirit, and can never be separated from our source, 'The Father,' which is LOVE."

Casey: "Woooo. The INsights of *The Butterfly Revelation* may, indeed, bring individuals a whole new kind of peace. I'm thinking, peace *of mind*. I am moving toward such peace of mind myself."

Idyllica: "Many *know about* peace of mind intellectually. I promise that, together, we are headed toward **knowing** a peace of mind that passes all understanding. The *Revelation* beacons will light the way. They will open the mind to a more sustaining and satisfying peace, a peace extending through and beyond the deepest and widest confines of one's spirit."

Casey: "I can hardly wait for The Caterpillar Club to gather tomorrow."

—⁓—

The Caterpillar Club is gathering. I wonder what today's discussion will be like. Mostly, I am excited because I know that whatever new scrawl fragment is introduced, I will have Idyllica, the spirit of the dazzling blue butterfly, to help me understand its meaning.

I am letting my own thoughts drift away. The leader today is Woolly Bear who is more exasperated than puzzled based upon the vibes I am getting. He is holding a leaf fragment whose surface has been decimated by a roaming band of aphids.

Woolly Bear seems uncertain. The slime writing seems to disappear into the ugly perforations that the aphids left behind.

———\//\\/\—

Woolly Bear is speaking. "The scrawl we have today may be complete and it may be incomplete. The thoughtless aphids ate holes into the leaf without realizing it held a priceless message. Are we ready for what I have translated?" As is the usual reaction, the seekers are wobble-nodding their readiness to get on with the discussion.

Your Eye Cannot See It 0 0 0 0

"What?!?" The entire group of caterpillar seekers seems truly baffled. "Our eye cannot see WHAT?" Unhappiness is clearly the mood of the moment.

Quickly, Woolly Bear's light hearted observation brings about an uplifting mood shift. "Well, I sometimes see more than I *want* to see, and sometimes more than I *ought* to see." The group chuckles. Woolly's timing is impeccable.

Woolly quizzically continues, "Who knows what all there is that I *cannot* see?" The perplexed seekers are now smiling.

Woolly Bear suggests a reasonable approach. "Let's think of things that we cannot see no matter how hard we try to see."

One after the other, the caterpillars offer possibilities. "How about things that are too small? You know, what we call 'no-see-ums.' We feel 'em even though we can't see 'em."

77

"How about things that are too big? I've heard about trees so tall that no caterpillar has ever reached the top leaves. I know I can't see something *that* big."

"I know something we can't see. We can't see something that is too far away."

"We can't see *anything* when we close our eyes!" The statement seems profound and stupid at the same time.

"So why are we wasting our time? Let's just close our eyes and answer the question. NOTHING! The eye that is closed sees NOTHING." The gatherers groan.

Woolly Bear breaks in, "I think we might very well be wasting precious time. No matter how many things we mention that we cannot see, we do not know if that is what the scrawl actually says. The wisdom of the message is what we seek to learn, is it not? Any ideas, anyone?" Woolly waits patiently.

Quiet. Hesitatingly, a whispered voice has everyone edging closer, "Maybe, just maybe, the subject is the eye itself and not what the ancient ones could see or what any of us might be able to see."

"What would that mean?" the suddenly curious Woolly Bear is prodding gently.

"I'm not sure. I am thinking that we may have given up too soon when we were urged to *Behold The Raindrop*. Because we have experienced rain storms, we did not really think very deeply about a single rain drop. This scrawl mentions a single eye. Rather than all the things we cannot see when we are looking, maybe our own eye is all we need to think about."

Woolly Bear misses the point. "So, there is something a single eye cannot see?"

Woolly is exasperated. "The hint is that we would learn about our life's purpose, our cocooning, and our destiny if we were to figure out what *one* eye cannot see? I'm afraid the aphids have hopelessly spoiled our fragment."

The seekers are once again wobble-nodding their agreement. The hesitant voice pleads against the consensus, "Not what does one eye *see*. What do we know about our own eye?" No one responds.

The hesitant voice tries one more time. "Isn't there some way to finish the statement that would help us know what the ancients were actually teaching? What, specifically, did the aphids chew away?"

No one is speaking. Woolly Bear begins sorting through the remaining leaf fragments. "Let's try another leaf. We seem to be at an impasse thanks to the aphids. It's a shame, I admit."

—⁓—

A gust of spirit fills my mind. It is as if my lungs are suddenly full even though I haven't taken a breath. Exhilarating! I **know** Idyllica is in the house!

Idyllica: "Ah, too bad. Your Caterpillar Club came oh so close to following the scrawl toward a grand INsight about our consciousness."

Casey: "Wahoo, you kept your promise to stay with me. Believe me, I really need you now. We have a problem. The INsight is too nebulous. There are a million things that the eye cannot see."

Idyllica: "No, my friend, no. The INsight is not nebulous. The fifth word is merely incomplete! The aphids obliterated part of the word. It just happens to be the key word."

Casey: "But the fragment says, 'your eye cannot see it.' The 'it' is missing. To me, that makes the whole thought nebulous."

Idyllica: "Incomplete! That's all. Incomplete. The fifth word is merely incomplete!"

Casey: "What, then, is the fifth word?"

Idyllica: "*It**SELF**. This scrawl is a very special truth about the mind. In its everyday conscious state, the mind cannot fully comprehend *itself*. Likewise, the healthy eye, when fully awake, sees nothing of *itself*."

Casey: "The healthy eye sees nothing of itself. Fascinating. That idea has never been brought to my attention. Yet, I find it to be a novelty thought rather than a special beacon, as you call it. Am I missing something? I do not understand."

Idyllica: "Once again, there is nothing to understand. Every *Revelation* INsight provides an unambiguous truism upon which to reflect. Each curious seeker discovers a meaning or an application that is specific to that individual's experience. A seemingly shallow, simple phrase may be quite deep with many levels of truth buried within it. The seeker finds only that wisdom which he or she is ready to understand."

Casey: "Sort of like a provocative parable or a once-upon-a-time-tale, if I may presume. With true wisdom stories, the listener is unconsciously engaged precisely at the point where his or her mind is most receptive. A too analytical listener desires a clean analogy, or perfect match, so that the story might fit the listener's predetermined notions of what is a good or poor example. Is this correct?"

Idyllica: "Yes, you are quite accurate about that. This is why you are the perfect translator for *The Butterfly Revelation.*"

Casey: "Thank you."

Idyllica: "You have learned to withhold your judgment when encountering something new. The majority of persons judge first. Later, many of these same persons realize that, by becoming opinionated too quickly, they had narrowed their perception and, thus, limited their understanding. Some hold on to their narrow opinions for a lifetime and are never aware that they might have lived a more full-filling life of the mind."

Casey: "My study of the wisdom of the sages convinces me that the subconscious mind absorbs the truth of a good wisdom tale, while the conscious mind argues its merits. Is that possible? That seems to be happening with my mind."

Idyllica: "Well said. Let's look at today's ages old observation, *Your Eye Cannot See Itself*, from two points-of-viewing. To the ophthalmologist or optometrist, a patient who sees something in his or her eye is a patient with a problem. The second point-of-viewing is from that portion of your own mind resting cell within cell inside the occipital lobe of the brain.

"I am referring simply to that part of yourself which 'sees' the physical world. A healthy eye is your spotless window."

Casey: "I once read a conclusion that captures this idea. The writer said, 'Death is the destruction of the body organ with which I see the world during my life; the destruction of the glass through which I look at this world. The destruction of the glass does not mean the destruction of the eye itself.' Am I getting the idea?"

Idyllica: "It might be a little more accurate to say, 'The destruction of the glass does not mean the destruction of see-er,' the mind that has been looking out through the glass."

Casey: "I am beginning to find a simple meaning within the thought that *Your Eye Cannot See Itself*."

[A contemplative pause]

Casey: "I am sensing that an acceptable affirmation of my potential for transformation would be to acknowledge that 'I' am NOT my eye. Neither am 'I' my ear, my tongue, or even my brain."

Idyllica: "Excellent. Take it one mini-step further. The true 'you' that is 'you' and no other, cannot be seen by you any more than your eye can see itself. The ancient ones who urged me to write this INsight were adamant that individuals not keep searching outside themselves for evidence of something they were clearly experiencing within themselves."

Casey: "Ah . . . One of our most famous philosophers certainly followed that advice by concluding, 'I think. Therefore, I am.' Is that in step with the advice of the butterfly ancients?"

Idyllica: "Quite in step, or 'in flutter,' as we say when two ideas share the same spirit."

Casey: "Am I 'in flutter' when I apply this eye INsight to earth life itself? Can I say that when my body, including my eyes, is no longer alive, and is no longer vibrating with terrestrial life, the main idea is that it is *only the body* and not 'I' that is no longer living?"

Idyllica: "Of course, you are referring to physical dying. There have been many attempts to clarify 'death,' which is what you long to understand. One of your own ancestors offered a word picture with which I especially flutter."

Casey: "I would love to know what flutters you."

Idyllica: "I commend this image: 'Death marks a change, it marks the disappearance of the dwelling place of your conscience. The conscience itself cannot be destroyed by death, in the same way as the change of a theater set cannot destroy the spectator.' What do you think?"

Casey: "I flutter with that, too."

Idyllica: "There is another word picture that I find interesting: 'The soul does not live in the body as in a house, but as in a tent, a place of temporary dwelling.' That certainly has been true for me."

Casey: "I also like that idea. Our time on earth does seem fleeting. Another of our philosophers remarked, 'Life is the remembrance of a very short day we spent visiting the earth.' This seems a common perspective among our more meditative ancestors."

Idyllica: "And ours."

Casey: "A very popular Roman, Marcus Aurelius, offered a similar notion reminding me that there have always been human seekers who would resonate with *The Butterfly Revelation*. This philosopher asked, 'Do you worry about the moment when you die? Our life is but a moment in eternity. Think and you will see that you have eternity behind you and before you, and between these two abysses, what difference does it make whether you live three days or three centuries?' He certainly accepted that who 'sees' is not the eye. Rather, who 'sees' is the one that *uses the eye* to see."

Idyllica: "You are fluttering with the spirit of today's beacon, it's light-giving INsight. Each thoughtful person will, sooner or later, come to his or her own point-of-view about what happens at the moment of death. Let me share one more human conclusion that, I must admit, I would have loved to have written myself."

Casey: "Please do."

Idyllica: "When I die, only one of two things can happen: either this essence which I understand as myself will transform into a different being, or I will stop being a separate individual and become a part of God. Either possibility is good."

Casey: "I recognize that perspective. Marcus Tullius Cicero was the one who said it."

Idyllica: "Yes it was he. To contemplate a bit more the invisibility of the mind that is 'you,' I have two additional subjects which mirror your soul's characteristic invisible vibration. Did you ever think that light itself is invisible? All of universal space is filled with dark, total blackness. Only when there is something which reflects light do we become aware of its existence."

Casey: "Light is invisible?!? It is everywhere yet cannot be seen? I'm flabbergasted."

Idyllica: "When you tire of pondering the idea of invisible light, think about the wind. It, too, is invisible. You do not see it, you only feel it and see what it stirs up.

"So, you see my friend, your consciousness (a.k.a. your mind, your soul, your being) is no more obscure than light and wind. Therefore, studying the actions of these life forces will yield new guidelines as to how consciousness may be used for the collective good of all men, all creatures, and all creation."

Casey: "Thanks for indwelling. Tomorrow is another Caterpillar Club gathering. May I expect your help?"

Idyllica: "We are inscrawlably united. I am enjoying this revisit to my own past."

—⁓—

Today there is a tempestuous wind which is whipping The Caterpillar Club canopy into a cataclysmic undulating leaf blanket. A creature isolated upon one of the leaves will survive only if it has a species specific stickiness that tenaciously adheres to the surface. Each leaf is tumbling, jerking, flipping and swooping as if it were an ingredient in a soup being stirred in a formless tureen by a mad chef.

Before the wind became so turbulent, the caterpillar seekers, huddling under the swaying branches, had chosen a *Butterfly Revelation* scrawl to analyze. Once again, I am baffled by the supposed value of a "wisdom fragment" which contains only three words:

Up Is Everywhere

I am not the only one baffled. I have cleared my mind and I am focusing on my friend, Monarchus IV. He, along with Woolly Bear, is determined to find meaning in the freshly translated squiggle.

Monarchus IV has a special charisma which all the seekers admire, none so adoringly as Pixie, whose heart palpitates at the mere thought of seeing him when the club convenes. Pixie is saddened to hear what Monarchus IV is saying.

"This leaf message," says Monarchus IV in a somewhat quavering voice, "may be the last one I am ever to contemplate. Each day I hope for some truth about our destiny. I have been diligent. I come with great expectations that I might learn what our ancestors discovered about the cocoon.

"Each day I leave hopelessly muddled about the true purpose of our munching, meandering, and cocooning, if there even is such a purpose."

Woolly Bear responds, "My friend, you returned from a near death experience. You discovered the fragments. You helped translate the messages. You inspired these friends to seek answers to questions that most caterpillars never ask. You led our first discussions. You have involved us in an unpredictable adventure. We have found companionship because of your curiosity. Your enthusiasm has helped us look beyond our everyday humdrum eating to survive. You have encouraged us to think about our destiny. By contemplating with us the mysterious scrawls, you are a lighthouse for us all. You must not let your light be dimmed."

"You are persuasive, Woolly, but I am tired of our dead-end gatherings. I am not a light. I am nothing more than a windblown creeper. Thankfully, today I am not up or I'd be blown down."

"You are more than a windblown creeper to us," Woolly is protesting. "You are a determined seeker, an adventurer, and we need to hear your thoughts about today's scrawl."

Monarchus IV speaks with calm deliberation, "I have a very real idea of where is 'up,' where is 'down,' where is 'left,' where is 'right,' where is 'here,' where is 'there,' where is 'in,' where is 'out,' and, to be perfectly honest, I have a very real idea about 'everywhere' as well. Today's message makes no sense. I'm sorry if it discourages anyone to hear me say that."

Woolly Bear is nearly blown over by a gust of wind. Woolly looks up and is alarmed. "I am concerned about the wind that is blowing our leaf umbrella every which way." Emphatically, Woolly adds, "Let's adjourn for today. But, Monarchus, I plead with you to come back tomorrow."

Woolly is appealing, hoping, grasping. "I feel there will be a wisdom breakthrough any day."

Woolly's voice is not convincing. However, on Woolly's face, his painful plea to Monarchus IV is written indelibly.

The caterpillars are scurrying to safety. Monarchus IV unexpectedly swivels his head around and surprisingly calls to Woolly Bear, "See ya tomorrow!"

⎯⤳⎯

I am intrigued with Monarchus IV's point-of-view. His thinking about here, there, and everywhere is similar to my own. I am delightedly relieved that he plans to meet with the club seekers again tomorrow. Naturally, I would not miss the next gathering for anything.

What annoys me is that I, too, cannot make heads nor tails of today's scrawl. My confusion is obvious. In the school of wisdom, today I feel like a kindergartener!

"I need you, Idyllica!"

Before I can even think the thought in words, the spirit of Idyllica fills my consciousness. I instantly *know* the butterfly spirit's mind-in-motion is fully integrated into my own mind.

Idyllica: "Ah, the futility of thinking about one's ultimate destiny as a specific location. It is an earth bound mental limitation. Before my own transformation, my metamorphosis, I had the exact limiting idea as Monarchus IV. I thought of all directions as locations. Had I never flown, I would not **know** today the simplicity and the truth of the observation, *Up Is Everywhere.*"

Casey: "Simplicity? Truth? I must be missing something."

Idyllica: "Here is a specific example. If you agree that I have offered an accurate description, you will immediately have a new perspective for all references to earth oriented directions."

Casey: "You know I like specifics. And, quite naturally, I am earth oriented. That is for sure."

Idyllica: "O.K., How about this? A sticky-footed caterpillar is clinging to the surface of a leaf. The caterpillar sees the sky 'above' and the earth 'below.' As the wind begins to blow, the leaf sways, flips and flops with every swirl, gust and puff of breeze. Get the picture?"

Casey: "Yes, it is a common occurrence. The wind blows and leaves are tossed about."

Idyllica: "Every twist of the leaf brings the caterpillar a new vision of 'up' and 'down.' At first, the sky is high over the leaf and the earth is underneath. During a gush of wind, the leaf is twisted completely upside-down."

Casey: "Excellent example. I have often seen stalwart tree limbs and spindly bush branches bend, twist, and flail back and forth during a nasty storm.

However, I never thought about the individual leaves and the insects hanging on to them for dear life."

Idyllica: "Let us think about them together. In such a storm, when the leaf is twisted completely upside-down, the earth is now 'above' the caterpillar, and the sky is 'below' the caterpillar and also 'below' the bottom of the leaf. While swirling and twisting, the direction of the leaf surface alternates among 'east' and 'west,' 'left' and 'right,' 'over this way' and 'over that way.'

"Every direction that is known and labeled will, at some moment in the caterpillar's frenzied whip-a-round, be located 'above' the caterpillar's back and/or 'below' the caterpillar's feet. I believe that you follow this truth."

Casey: "I am with you. Indeed, I see that up and down do change for the caterpillar, especially during an unexpected wind storm."

Idyllica: "Now, then, the simple truth of the *Revelation* statement is revealed. *Up Is Everywhere*! For the caterpillar, 'up' depends entirely upon where he or she is standing when asked, 'Which way is up?' I sense that you see this truth in the wind-storm word picture."

Casey: "Oh, oh, oh, yes. I get it. Up IS Everywhere! And a special word picture has just occurred to me."

Idyllica: "I already love your example. For your future readers, go right ahead and think out the words that will help them understand the power of this true saying to explain, among other things, exactly where 'heaven' is."

Casey: "Suppose someone were standing on a star speaking to three persons each of whom is standing at a different spot on the earth. One is standing at the North Pole. One is standing at the South Pole. The third is standing on the earth at a point along the equator. The person on the star asks, 'Which way is up?' All three persons on the earth immediately point directly over their heads."

Idyllica: "And . . ."

Casey: "They are pointing in three *different* directions!!"

Idyllica: "And . . . "

Casey: "Up Is Everywhere! It all depends upon where you are standing when you are asked the question."

Idyllica: "The ancient discerners of butterfly wisdom, upon beginning to fly, had discovered this very truth. What had been truth in living their earthbound lives no longer explained their experience while living their airborne lives. For a flying creature, what was up or down became part of a game. 'There' could be 'here' with just a few wing flaps. 'Up' could be 'down' under the feet, with a simple roll-over maneuver. The answer to 'Where am I?' needed new words!"

Casey: "Wow, this is exciting. After transformation, old ways of describing where one 'is' become misleading, or even obsolete."

Idyllica: "Quite clearly. Commonly accepted meanings of words actually prevent any caterpillar seeker from knowing where he or she might expect to be after the transition from a creeping life to a flying life.	The use of words with currently accepted meanings also interferes with learning what one might expect, and where one might be, after the glorious flutteration which supersedes death."

Casey: "What might the beacon, *Up Is Everywhere*, reveal to humans that is currently being obscured by accepted meanings of words?	Does this scrawl actually clarify the location of heaven for humans?"

Idyllica: "This INsight, more than any other, says that heaven is not a place.	The earthbound idea that heaven is 'up,' continues to obscure the truth that heaven is *everywhere*.	As one revered teacher boldly stated, 'The kingdom of heaven is *at hand*.' He might just as well have said, *within*, or *everywhere*.	Heaven, you see, is not a place."

Casey: "I want to know more."

Idyllica: "The most well known of biblical prayers, *The Lord's Prayer*, suggests the same truth.	Addressing the all embracive source of life as Father, the prayer casually observes, 'Our Father which art *in heaven* . . .' A couple clauses later, the prayer makes another observation.	Some think the statement is a wish, a hope, or a kind of plea which is being uttered.	Rather, I offer you an alternative conclusion.	The words of the prayer contain a quite simple truth.	It is a straightforward statement of *the way life is*."

Casey: "What is the telltale statement?	I have repeated the words of this prayer throughout my life. I must admit that many times I just say the words without experiencing anything special."

Idyllica: "Yes, that is your terrestrial mind at work, your caterpillar understanding, if I may say so without insulting you."

Casey: "I am not insulted. Frankly, I feel loved when I become aware that you are within my mind. I **know** that you are guiding me toward greater understanding of both the here and the hereafter of earth life."

Idyllica: "Consider, then, the miracle of life everlasting which lies slightly obscured behind these next few words of *The Lord's Prayer*: '. . . Thy kingdom come. Thy will be done, on earth as it is in heaven . . .' Anyone praying this prayer is acknowledging with these words that the mind of the one praying accepts the truth that whatever LOVE is to be manifest on the earth, that 'love' will be brought forth from within the heart of the one praying."

Casey: "That is what many call an 'affirmation.' What is done on earth originates within the mind and heart of man. I get that. I am not so clear about 'as it is in heaven.' Help me."

Idyllica: "Anywhere, everywhere, and any time that heaven is expressed on earth, it is because the vibration of heavenly LOVE has temporarily superseded the congestion and ordinary clutter of the earthly focused mind."

Casey: "I need to digest this explanation. I want to quiet my mind. I shall abandon words. I am suddenly overwhelmed with the funny notion that I may have 'bitten off more than I can chew' here today."

Idyllica: "I, too, shall remain wordless for a little while. You are very close to clearly expressing one of the truths that will bring peace of mind to anyone who receives it."

[The moments that passed at this point may have been few or many. I have no way of knowing.]

Casey: (contemplating) "The sense I am getting is so different from the traditional ideas that I have been taught about heaven. My understanding at this moment is simply that heaven is not somewhere else. One does not 'go to heaven' upon the decease of the terrestrial body.

"At this moment, I also understand that any person, while very much alive, can tune into heaven. Heaven is *at hand*. Heaven may be fully engaged through the stilling of the mind."

Idyllica: (engaging) "Just as up is everywhere, the wise ones do affirm that heaven is everywhere. Thus, one can *enter* heaven, even communicating with long departed souls, just as we are communicating. This is done by getting in tune with the infinite, immeasurable, omnipresent celestial vibration while tuning out most delimiting, sluggish, terrestrial vibrations. Upon the demise of the body, the mind discards its restricting terrestrial 'temple' altogether and acquires its boundless celestial 'mansion' instantaneously."

Casey: "I have a new sense that earthly death simply removes all barriers, all mental blocks, all human thought patterns that during earth living effectively obscure a **knowing** of the unity of life, the presence of the Holy Spirit, and the unfathomable LOVE of The Father. I must say I have a wonderfully expanded appreciation of 'up.' And, at this point, I really need to get in tune with the poet, David, the psalm-composing shepherd boy who became a king."

Idyllica: "Why is that?"

Casey: In my mind, along with the poet, I want to *lie down in green pastures* fully conscious of the Father and the creative power within myself. I want to be *led beside still waters* and be refreshed from their bottomless reservoirs of Love. I want the Holy Spirit to *restore my soul* to its full capacity for expressing peace in a conflicted world."

Idyllica: "I am delighted. The messages of *The Butterfly Revelation* are churning beautifully in your very soul."

Casey: "I can hardly wait for The Caterpillar Club gathering tomorrow and *The Butterfly Revelation* scrawl of the day."

———

The violent wind storm is no more. As treacherous as the straining branches and the swirling leaves were for all climbing caterpillars yesterday, today the air is calm and the leaf canopy over the caterpillar meeting place is completely tranquil. Sunshine and shadows warm and cool each seeker as he or she wriggles leisurely side to side.

I sense a mood of calm longing. The friends greet each other with expressions of relief and curiosity. "Whew, that was some wind blaster yesterday, eh?"

95

"Yes, indeed. And it was a Topsy-Turvy fragment, as well." "I'm thinking that with the sunshine today we might have a scrawl that brings new light." "Ah, let's hope."

———

All the regular caterpillar seekers have arrived. The group, especially Woolly Bear, seems genuinely happy to see Monarchus IV. It is Monarchus IV who begins the discussion.

"I apologize for my frustration yesterday. I have had a full night and day to reflect on all that we have been struggling to learn. The INsights from *The Butterfly Revelation* are proving to be more obscure than I had imagined they would be. I did not mean to discourage anyone else. In fact, the alternative to continuing the struggle to learn is to give up. I tried that once and almost did not survive. I will not give up. That is my promise. I am ready, Woolly, for today's leaf."

Woolly Bear has shuffled the remaining few leaf fragments into a slightly skewed stack. Nodding to Lawrence, whose risk-taking style is described earlier in this notebook, Woolly invitingly nudges the stack toward the center of the group. Lawrence, The Emperor, not hesitating, attaches a sticky footpad to the edge of a leaf fragment which is tucked slightly under the others. He tugs the leaf free.

The fragment has three large well preserved words and some other smaller squiggled words which are partially riddled with annoying aphid holes.

Trust The Cocoon
gat0way t0 0he 0ky life

To the caterpillar seekers, the word "cocoon" is akin to the human word "death." There is mystery. There is the unknown. There is finality. There is disappearance. There is loss. There is grieving. There is nothing. "Here today, gone tomorrow," is a quip that is as familiar to my insect friends as it is to my human friends.

"Gone where?" Ah, that is always a contentious question. Some humans demand observation and so-called "facts" even when speaking about the "afterlife." For others, these demands are pushed aside by speculation and so-called "contacts" from those who are "on the other side."

I am interested not only in what the seekers may discover today, but also in what I might learn from Idyllica who has promised to remain permeated with me. (Come to think of it, I guess the spirit of Idyllica qualifies as a "contact from the other side," doesn't it?)

The cocoon fragment is immediately energizing to the club. Each caterpillar is inexorably driven to create a cocoon, a seeming tomb. Consequently, the cocoon is an unwelcome subject of conversation in most caterpillar clans. To find the term, cocoon, central to a wisdom scrawl has stirred the seekers in a way that I have not seen before. The gatherers seem desperate to know more about the cocoon. Emotion is brimming. We humans would say a "buzz" is beginning.

"I can't wait to learn something, *anything*, about the cocoon!" I pick up this sentiment simultaneously from three, perhaps four, of the caterpillars who have squirmed even closer to the center of the circle, close enough to peek at the main message, *Trust The Cocoon*. Woolly and Monarchus IV are curled directly above the leaf eager to read the entire message.

Together, the two leaders determine that after allowing for normal spacing there may be four letters that have been obliterated by the surgical chewing of the aphids. The others are invited to help fill in the blanks: *gat_way t_ _he _ky life*.

Everyone is riveted. *gat_way t_ _he _ky life*. Hmmm . . .

I think I know what letters are missing. After a couple minutes, I am certain that the *Butterfly Revelation* message reads: *Trust The Cocoon . . . gateway to the sky life*.

The Caterpillar Club is teetering on the edge of a breakthrough. If I am correct, the entire statement offers to caterpillars a new definition of purpose for the cocoon. For me and other humans who are intrigued by a caterpillar's transformation into a butterfly, the scrawl analogously suggests to us a different purpose for death itself. Death is not, of itself, the termination of life. Hmmm . . .

A "gateway" between terrestrial and celestial ways of living seems a much grander way to describe the moment of death than the somewhat morbid notion that death is one's "ticket to the tomb." I am thrilled to think of the difference.

I want the caterpillars to experience the exhilaration that a simple change of focus can bring to the mind. INsight often can excite.

Some would argue that changing words does not change truth. However, with this new INsight before me, I would argue that reflecting upon "terrestrial/celestial" and "tomb/gateway" is much, much more than merely changing words.

I love the idea of "sky life" for unsuspecting caterpillar creepers. I also love the idea of a "gateway" for human transcendence rather than a "tomb" conveying the notion that burying the body marks a human "final resting place." Let's learn how the caterpillars respond.

Woolly Bear, having excelled during his school years in the fine achievement of literary analysis, raises his head and announces what he has decoded. "The most common word in our language includes 'he' and is preceded with a 't'. That word is 'the'. The only three letter word that has the letters 'ky' is a wonder filled word. That word is 'sky'! The only two letter word that begins with the letter 't' is the word 'to'. So, we may be assured that the message reads as follows: *Trust The Cocoon gat_way TO THE SKY LIFE.*"

"What about the other missing letter, Woolly?" An attentive seeker speaks for everyone.

"I am considering the options," Woolly is answering slowly, thoughtfully. "The letters 'w-a-y' may be preceded by the letter 'a' or the letter 's' or possibly an 'x' where a crossing or an unknown direction is being indicated. I am not absolutely certain which to choose."

Monarchus IV speaks up, "I am focused on the letters 'g-a-t' and cannot think of any word beside the word 'gather' in which 'g-a-t' is followed by a letter other than 'e'. Since we know that 'w-a-y' is clearly. . . Whoa! Yo! Heigh Ho! I've got it! The word is 'GATEWAY' without a doubt. The missing letter is the letter 'e'. Everybody, read it now."

I am hearing what sounds somewhat like the chant with which the Caterpillar Club sessions usually begin. The blended voices reverberate. The small ensemble is singing and swaying.

Trust The Cocoon
gateway to the sky life

There is an exuberance in the sound that resonates from one seeker to and through another. With each repetition of the "cocoon refrain" the group seems to reach a new high.

I am reminded of the intoxication that often accompanies repeated drumming or ritual cheering among my human friends. There is, as yet, no effort by the caterpillars to discern the *meaning* of the message. The chanted words themselves appear to carry a *subconsciously recognizable* INsight that is immediately reflected in a joyous demeanor. Every caterpillar seeker is affected. Oddly, the cocoon chant is upbeat, contagious.

Slowly, the scrawl inspired song is dwindling, fading, vanishing. There is a new sort of quiet, a kind of hush, that is affecting every one of the now worn-out singers. This is a new experience for the group.

Completely unaware, the gatherers have been drawn into a rare contemplative state. Each mind seems "open" to a degree that would be unthinkable to any caterpillar who has not been meeting regularly, frustratingly, steadfastly committed to discovering the truth about the cocoon.

The group is quiet, trancelike, "spaced out," barely conscious, enthralled. I, too, have been caught up in the near hypnotic effect of the prolonged period of chanting. The rhythm has been infectious; however, I am now focusing upon the words. I want to understand the meaning of the words that Woolly and the other caterpillars are ready to contemplate.

I wait for the club itself to tackle the idea. *Trust The Cocoon* is the scrawl's instruction, its primary advice. As determined by Woolly Bear and Monarchus IV, *gateway to the sky life,* is the secondary message smeared on the leaf fragment.

The word, cocoon, is modified somewhat enigmatically by the scrawl. The ancient *Revelation* wisdom phrase gives the cocoon a *function.* I sense the group is ready, ready and open-minded. There is stirring. A low key discussion is beginning.

Vanessa is speaking. "A gateway, for sure, is NOT a dead end. I have wondered why every caterpillar in my family works so hard and eats so much just to be able to spin a cocoon. When I ask, I am always told that it is an old custom to prepare the finest final resting place possible. Nothing more is ever explained. 'It is the caterpillar way,' I am assured. Several of my family have bellowed at me, 'SHUT UP AND EAT!' I quit asking."

"The very same thing has happened to me," three of the seekers speak and nod simultaneously.

"What, then, do *you* think when you hear the word 'gateway' since you do not think of a dead end?" asks the diplomatic Woolly Bear as he turns toward Vanessa.

Thoughtfully, the always sincere Vanessa says, "To me, a gateway is something that one enters on one side, goes through, and departs from the other side. Or, depending upon how it is constructed, a gateway is simply a structure that is entered at one point and exited from another point."

"Ah," Woolly summarizes, "You would be thinking that while a completed cocoon is something that one enters, the same cocoon is also a structure that one might leave. Correct?"

Vanessa has a quizzical look, "I never, ever imagined that a cocoon is something that one would leave. Today's idea comes as a total surprise to me."

Vanessa is deliberating out loud. "That a cocoon might be a gateway is an idea I have never heard before. And, *gateway to the sky* is, at this moment, completely inconceivable. All I have ever heard about sky is that the birds fly there. Sky and caterpillar just don't jibe."

Monarchus IV, excitedly, "Hey, listen everybody! Today we have an ancient proposition that connects flying with cocoons. We all intend to build cocoons. So, we connect with this scrawl . . . don't we? Or, is flying just a dumb dream, and we are dummies?"

Every caterpillar gatherer is fully attentive to Monarchus IV. He is exuding high energy. His charismatic appeal has never been more obvious.

Monarchus IV continues. "Well, let me tell you what I just remembered. When I stopped eating and was about to perish, I had what I think was a dream. In the dream, I was reminded of an ages-old, Monarchus Clan notion that I thought was gibberish. *You were born to fly* was the dream notion."

Pixie, who keeps a record of the important pronouncements made during the caterpillar gatherings, quickly seeks clarity. "Explain the connection between cocoons and flying, please."

"Well," says Monarchus IV, "the only way to travel in the sky is to fly. If both propositions are truly wisdom statements, we caterpillars are someday going to fly. That *seems* impossible to us. But what if something happens inside the cocoon that we have never been told? What if we change in some way rather than simply disappearing from sight?"

Monarchus IV is ruminating openly. "What if there *is* a way out of the cocoon? What if the cocoon actually *is* a point-of-passage, a gateway? What if we continue to live both inside and beyond the cocoon? What if both ideas are true?"

Pixie is wide-eyed, "Is there a way to express what you are speculating?"

"There IS a word," Monarchus IV is searching for just the right thing to say, "and I have never before used it to describe anything about our caterpillar lives. Somehow, the word is related to something else I was told in my near-death dream."

103

"What is the word?" Pixie is beguiled by Monarchus IV and his possible answer. Pixie has always been enamored of the messenger. Now, she seems equally fascinated by the yet unspoken message.

"Transformation. Yes, transformation. That is the impression I received. In the cocoon, it is possible that each of us might be *transformed*. I cannot say what the word means precisely."

Pixie is noting the word and continues probing, "What additional impressions did you receive?"

"I remember a single idea which I disregarded at the time. I could not see how the idea would apply to me. Now, I realize, I was being given a sort of indescribable 'hope' intended to restore my desire to eat my way back to healthy caterpillar living."

Pixie loved the way Monarchus IV walked and talked. Even more, she loved the way he seemed always to know things that the other seekers did not. "Please, I would love to know what idea had such a life saving effect upon you. Would you tell us?"

"The greatest creeping is less magnificent than the poorest flying."

Monarchus IV seems pleased with himself as he shares his memory. He also seems surprised, a "lightbulb moment."

All the seekers are murmuring and looking at one another as if they have opened a precious package and are not sure just what to do with it. One by one, each caterpillar is making the connection that Monarchus IV made just moments earlier. Creeping and flying, is the cocoon actually a bridge of some sort between the two?

104

Once again, Woolly Bear, the superior synthesizer, provides perspective, "We certainly agree that we are, every one of us, creepers. Some, honestly, are much more gifted in creeping than others. A few of us have a distinctive, I would say a magnificent style, which is much admired in our community. Are we agreed?"

Wobble-nodding, scrunching-unscrunching, antenna-wiggling, all support the chorus, "Yes."

Woolly Bear is continuing, "Now, we have earlier agreed that, regardless of the intriguing statement, *You were born to fly*, no caterpillar has ever flown, nor would we ever expect one to fly. Is this true?" Woolly sees unanimous ring-around consensus wobble-nodding, scrunching-unscrunching, antenna-wiggling.

"So," Woolly is summarizing, "the ancient seers are hinting that something might happen inside the cocoon that changes everything we know and believe about our destiny. Each of us might be transformed in some unthinkable way."

Woolly, too, is now having a lightbulb moment. "The result of that transformation would be the ability to use the cocoon as a gateway, a mere way station, for a life that would continue *in the sky*! It is both breathtaking and unfathomable to me."

"Yes," Monarchus IV is adding, "and the problem is that flying would require a whole new body structure for us. We have been ideally made for creeping, even magnificent creeping. Yet, we certainly know from observing the birds, the dragonflies, the bees and the butterflies, to travel from a near place to a far place, the very poorest flying is, indeed, well beyond what the most magnificent creeper among us can accomplish."

"So?" It is Woolly Bear with a raised brow.

"So," Monarchus IV is concluding, "Each of us would need to develop a completely new body structure while inside the cocoon. We would need to emerge from a so-called cocoon gateway with a body that could fly." There is a long, breathless pause. "Sorry. I think such a thing is *impossible*. However, I will give the ancients credit. The gateway scrawl is my favorite so far."

Today, the Caterpillar Club is the most animated I have witnessed. The gathering has had a new openness, a shifted mood, an hypnotic attraction, and, above all, a *Revelation* fragment that finally provides a substantive subject rather than the usual esoteric puzzle message.

There is visible collective deflation, however, as Monarchus IV wriggles slowly away. The charisma, so obvious moments earlier, faded when Monarchus IV said that he, personally, did not think it possible that the required transformation of body structure could take place inside a cocoon.

It is as if Monarchus IV has punctured a balloon inflated with "pipe dreams." The seekers' enthusiasm is completely deflated.

———

The idea of the cocoon as a gateway is a lure that appeals to me. I am not ready to stop thinking about cocoons, tombs, and death as being gateways. I am bursting with curiosity!

I feel that I am on the cusp of finding out something very important about the transition from life through death to the afterlife. Certainly, Idyllica will have some INsight into the gateway scrawl's deeper messages. Come quickly, spirit friend.

The breathless rush of breath . . . Idyllica!

Idyllica: "Good day, friend Casey. Did you notice what just happened with Monarchus IV? As with you humans, minds will shut down when a conclusion is reached prematurely. When it is a faulty conclusion, the shut down is especially disheartening."

Casey: "No, I am not sure what happened. What premature conclusion? What faulty conclusion? And, what does 'minds will shut down' mean?"

Idyllica: "Monarchus IV announced, 'I think such a thing is *impossible.*' There is no surer way to distract your attention and give the mind *something else* upon which to focus.

"Once you have declared something 'impossible,' your mind will automatically disregard anything that might be helpful in proving otherwise. No caterpillar, including Monarchus IV, can imagine the changes they will undergo in the cocoon. If they concur with the word 'impossible,' they shut off any chance of **knowing** the truth."

Casey: "Have the caterpillars no chance of learning their true nature? Will they never embrace the idea that they were born to fly? Does contemplating the *Revelation* INsights ever lead to new hope or stronger faith or deeper trust in what might lie beyond the cocoon?"

Idyllica: "First, the state of mind that each caterpillar develops as he or she gets closer to the time of cocooning makes a world of difference. The difference is in how ambitiously each prepares, and how enthusiastically each looks forward to the mysterious time that follows the moment of being encapsulated fully in one's own cocoon.

"You humans, too, have very different thoughts and feelings about burying or incinerating the body in which you have been having your soul experiences. The differences are quite often directly related to what you have considered *possible* or *impossible*."

Casey: "To say something is *possible* or *impossible* is merely an opinion. Are you saying humans and caterpillars can never **know** their true inherent destiny? Must we play mind games in order to view our own deaths as somehow desirable?

"I do not understand how Monarchus IV could **know** what lies beyond the cocoon, or, in my case, **know** what lies beyond the grave. All we have are our opinions. Isn't it better to at least *think* some life beyond is *possible*?"

Idyllica: "You have, as yet, not been introduced to all *The Butterfly Revelation* INsights that have the potential to inform your mind of the what, who, where, and how of your own eternal nature. I expect that you will **know** enough before I leave you that you will have not only greater hope, faith, and trust, but also much greater peace. Peace of mind is priceless. Yet, it is free!"

Casey: "I do not wish to be rude. However, I must urge you to get back to specific, practical ways of explaining what you can about life hereafter. I believe that you are 'alive.' I do *know* that. Others will speculate about our relationship. If they conclude that for the two of us to be united in spirit is *impossible*, their thinking will be shut off at some early point in our story. So be it."

Idyllica: "O.K., fair request, and I do not think you rude for wanting to learn."

Casey: "Thanks. Now on with the simplified version. Keep sharing what you *know* about our eternal nature, if you would, please."

Idyllica: "I begin by sharing what I shall call a hidden truth. This basic truth is unknown to even the wisest butterfly. In fact, no living butterfly can ever *know* this! I repeat, the truth of this hidden INsight' is unknowable to any living butterfly, regardless of age, experience, or desire to understand."

Casey: "That certainly qualifies as hidden. Is it the same for humans? How can I *know* an unknowable truth?"

Idyllica: "Well, the most basic wisdom INsight for humans only seems unknowable . . . initially."

Casey: "I am captivated by the thought of learning a hidden truth. First, however, refresh my thinking about the INsight you describe as 'the most basic wisdom INsight for humans.' For the moment I was focused completely on butterfly thinking."

Idyllica: "O.K. Let's review. Basic to caterpillar truth seeking is the assertion, *You were born to fly*. Basic to human truth seeking is the often overlooked premise, *You were born to transcend.* Transcendence to celestial living is your natural heritage, not some prize that you would need to earn, or a special dispensation available only to a select few among all humans."

Casey: "Oh, indeed, I am with you concerning the caterpillar destiny claim. The overlooked human premise is somewhat obscure to me and I want to return to it in a moment. For now, let's stay with the secret butterfly wisdom. I am deeply curious as to what you might share with me. Perhaps you have a practical word picture, that I can mull over."

Idyllica: "For the record, let us begin with the idea that the goal is to **know**. Mulling things over only sometimes leads to full **knowing**.

"Now, pay close attention. I strongly caution you and your eventual readers, mulling can become mental gymnastics, a kind of exercise that simply enables participants to get better and better at mulling things over. Some discussion groups bounce the same ideas back and forth, over and over, merely going 'round the *mull*-berry bush."

Casey: "I will heed that caution. Now, for the wisdom, eh?"

Idyllica: "Cocooning is for *changing one's clothes.* The image of a closet might come to mind."

Casey: "It does."

Idyllica: "Dying is for *taking off one's clothes.*"

Casey: "I am flabbergasted. I can hardly breathe. I think I have just absorbed the difference between *transformation* and *transcendence.*"

Idyllica: "You have, indeed. You have NOW been initiated. Let me hear what words you will put to your new understanding.   You *know* the secret understanding about my very existence!"

Casey: (utterly astonished) "Idyllica, you have experienced both *transformation* and *transcendence*!"

Idyllica: "Bingo!"

Casey: "Earlier, in my notebook, it was explained to me that humans may change much about themselves while experiencing terrestrial life. These changes may seem quite transforming even though they are fully terrestrial living changes. These changes are merely shadows of the changes a caterpillar experiences.

"Humans do not have a metamorphosis comparable to that which caterpillars undergo. We ought not, therefore, think of our transition to life-after-life as simply a special kind of terrestrial transformation that, somehow, is a bit more grandiose than the process of a caterpillar becoming a butterfly. Am I on track?"

Idyllica: "Good. Please continue. You are about to offer something quite wise to those who struggle to create human dogma that likens aging with caterpillar metamorphosis thus creating a happy ending to their life stories.

"Simplified, humans are often told to think of themselves as caterpillars becoming butterflies rather than dying. But, of course, *butterflies also die!*"

Casey: "Well, I am flabbergasted because I realize now that you, Idyllica, are not communicating as a mere butterfly, a *transformed* caterpillar.

"YOU ARE 'SPIRIT,' THE VERY ESSENCE OF A *DEAD* BUTTERFLY!"

Idyllica: "Bingo, again."

Casey: "Which means, oh my goodness, that you have unquestionably experienced *transcendence* as well as *transformation*!

Idyllica: "You now **know** something profoundly enlightening. The same **knowing** has been discovered by other determined, truth-seeking, earth bound living souls, and is quite simple.

"Transcendence occurs only when the terrestrial 'home of the soul' is no longer alive, vibrating, imprisoning, what humans refer to as DEAD. However, there are well-known exceptions."

Casey: "There are exceptions to dying?!?"

Idyllica: "No, no. There are not exceptions to dying. I speak of the exceptions which make it possible, while living, for someone to experience transcendence, to **know** what lies beyond dying.

Casey: "Beyond dying? We can experience transcendence while alive? I am eager the know about these exceptions. "

Idyllica: "Under certain conditions, two of which are deep meditative trance and massive physical trauma, the recognizable soul escapes for a time from the constraints of the disengaged body. At these times, an individual may experience, at first hand, some wide ranging *transcendent living* phenomena.

"These episodes are described by some writers as 'out-of-body experiences,' alluded to by others as 'enlightenment,' and by others as mere 'moments of celestial living.' By any label, these are *transcendent* experiences."

Casey: "So, am I correct in concluding that when a caterpillar is transformed, becoming a butterfly, the caterpillar and the butterfly are, in essence, the same living creature?"

Idyllica: "Precisely. From a spiritual point-of-viewing, the two earthly manifestations are both expressions of the same living soul. The experiences of both caterpillar and butterfly are merely the inhalation and exhalation of the loving Father in a restricted time-and-place environment named 'earth' by humans."

Casey: "Whoa! A living butterfly's spirit is just as time-and-place encumbered as that of a caterpillar, having merely been transformed, easing from one earthly 'home' into another earthly 'home' by means of metamorphosis. The cocoon, then, is a gateway, NOT to celestial living, but from living as a creeper to living as a flyer . . . on earth!"

Idyllica: "Bingo!"

Casey: "But you! What about you?"

Idyllica: "You already **know**. You **know** me. The additional truth that you are now ready to absorb is that when we are together, you are experiencing 'heaven.' You **know** that I, dazzling blue flyer of the Peleides family, have not just *changed* clothes, I have *taken off* my terrestrial clothes. I have *transcended* my earth-confining, blue winged body, lovely as it was."

Casey: "Whooooo, this is breathtaking."

Idyllica: "Yes, breathtaking, but not unheard of. Indeed, your wisdom teachers have used other terms for the soul's terrestrial and celestial natures."

Casey: "Other words describing the terrestrial and celestial?"

Idyllica: "We will come back to such words. Regardless, the fact remains that whatever you choose for the word pictures that convey our present *knowing*, this moment's truth is that you and I are both alive, now and for eternity. The INsight, *now and eternity are one and the same*, is no longer vague. We are experiencing now and eternity together.

"You *know* at this moment what for many will, regrettably, remain hidden, simply UN*known*, because, by filing the notion away as *impossible*, they shut off their minds to the possibility that the INsight is a true saying."

Casey: "Regrettable is not the same as irreversible, is it?"

Idyllica: "Not at all the same, though it is discouraging to observe that so many humans cling to their self-determined 'impossibilities' and remain close-minded when they could enjoy the fruits of being open-minded by merely filing some new ideas as 'possibilities.' No individuals have to abandon their beliefs, or reverse their comfortable conclusions, to merely *consider* the possible.

"We need only change our beliefs when we *expand our experience* **and** *know* **that our former beliefs can no longer hold what we have discovered to be true."**

Casey: "I want to be one who considers new possibilities and explanations for what our lives might be like beyond what we call 'life on earth.' For instance, to what other wisdom terms for our terrestrial and celestial natures did you refer?"

Idyllica: "One Holy Scripture describes the terrestrial body as a temple. I like that."

Casey: "Ah yes, blessed and consecrated. Nothing mysterious there. I do know that humans treat temples with great reverence and expect to encounter God's Spirit upon entering the doorway. To me, temple is a meaningful word picture for body when you accept that heaven is always *at hand*."

Idyllica: "Well reasoned. However, I prefer the idea of the philosopher whom I earlier quoted who said that on earth we live as in a tent. Unlike elaborately constructed temples which suggest a permanent earthly existence, the word 'tent' expresses the simple acknowledgement that our spirit-soul nature is only briefly ensconced on the earth plane of living. We are *temporary* bodily tent dwellers."

Casey: "What about a celestial word picture? Do you have a favorite?"

Idyllica: "I like one especially. When the earth tent exists no more, whether human or butterfly, a celestial 'mansion' is required. It must be a glorious mansion so that it might be home to a soul that is no longer bound by time and space. It must be different from a home for an earth-confined body."

Casey: "So, I am thinking that this mansion is not really a place or a dwelling. Is this right?"

Idyllica: "I can tell you from my point-of-viewing, the spiritual mansion is unlike anything a human might imagine. You must set aside almost all earth notions of dwelling. My mansion and the one you will inherit have been prepared from beyond the beginning of time and space as humans understand those terms."

Idyllica (The tone of a trusted confidant): "A master teacher, Jesus of Nazareth, identifying his own spirit as that of the Creator's spirit, indicated a mansion has been prepared for those who listened to His teaching and 'if it were not so, I would have told you.' I, myself, now live in such a mansion, a state of existence that has exceeded any notion that I had as a butterflying soul."

Casey (The rapt attention of a devotee): "Tell me what you can about your eternal mansion existence."

Idyllica: "Any celestial mansion must have room for all the spirit-that-has-ever-existed. It must be a home that is boundless since the inhabitant will no longer be earth bound. At the moment of terrestrial death, 'earth to earth, dust to dust', the boundless, timeless abode must receive its new occupant in such a way that the transitioning soul *knows*, 'I am FREE. I am FREE TO BE ME!' I am home. I *know* I am on the same creative plane with the Father and can explore every nook and cranny of creation."

Casey: "That does not sound like a true structure of any kind. This description of mansion seems to paint a picture of a new kind of awareness, not a new kind of building."

Idyllica: "You are resonating perfectly in sync with the very heart of *The Butterfly Revelation.*"

Casey: "How is that?"

Idyllica: "You infer a special INsight from the ancient *Revelation* fragments. **Heaven is *direct knowing!* Heaven is both a state of being and a state of becoming. Heavenly is what you *become*, not where you go!**

"Your celestial nature is boundless and everlasting. Heaven includes every one of the infinite 'wave lengths' of creation, all of which are available to a heavenly being."

Casey: "Such as the wave length that we are using this very moment."

Idyllica: "Such as the wave length that we are CREATING this very moment."

Casey: "Creating?"

Idyllica: "Precisely. We are not only *using* a specific vibratory pattern, wave length in common human usage, but also, during every passing moment, we are *creating* new variations which become a part of all creation. We, my friend, are created in the image of a Creator. We, then, are creating a 'new heaven and a new earth' with every moment of our being!"

Casey: "Oh, me. Oh, my. This entire day is too much for me to absorb. Briefly, I grasped the deeper meaning of the pronouncement, *Trust The Cocoon . . . gateway to the sky life.* Using the familiar idea of a gateway, I realized the difference between transformation and transcendence. To be sure, my mind is boggled by the simplicity of the mental awakening I experienced as you expressed the distinction between *changing your terrestrial clothes*, which you did in a cocoon of your own making, and *taking off your terrestrial clothes*, which you did when your butterfly body reverted to earth dust from which it had been created. But now, my spirit friend, I am overwhelmed."

Idyllica: "How so?"

Casey: "As boggled as I was by the truth that heavenly describes what you become, not where you go, this latest notion that I am a creator made in the image of the Creator-Of-All-Creation goes way beyond what I can grasp upon first encountering the possibility of its truth."

Idyllica: "Do not shut down your mind just yet."

Casey: "Alright, but I really, really need your help."

Idyllica: "Let's try just one 'realization' before we rest for today. Where would you like to start?"

Casey: "O.K., good enough, one more . . . Let's take the simple correction you just made. You informed my mind that we are not merely *using* a wavelength. You conveyed that we are also *creating* a wavelength. I gather the obvious meaning. What we are experiencing together has its own existence, its own vibrational pattern, its own distinct time and place here on earth. Then, you expanded the concept far beyond anything I have ever thought before.

"You revealed that we, you in the celestial realm and I on the terrestrial level, together, are 'creating a new heaven and a new earth.' Help me get this clearer in my mind, and clearer for the eventual readers of this notebook."

Idyllica: "Gladly, for there is nothing cloudy about the idea or its truth."

Casey: "Nothing cloudy to you, perhaps."

Idyllica: "Creation is continuously expanding. Every at-this-moment action, feeling and thought, what you think of as 'new,' is building this expanding creation. Simply, we help create creation."

Casey: "Does 'we' really mean 'we on earth' as well as your 'we in heaven'?"

Idyllica: "Clearly summarized, my friend, though you made it a question."

Casey: "Thank you, but I don't actually know what I was thinking."

Idyllica: "Try this idea. Then, we will separate for awhile.

"Whether terrestrial or celestial, creation is expanding. All matter, including the known and unknown to humans, the discovered and undiscovered, the local manifestation and that which appears a million galaxies away, is in constant motion. If there were no attraction, no 'glue,' there would be chaos rather than an orderly creation."

Casey: "There must be something to hold all creation together. Is this correct? Am I with you?"

Idyllica: "Indeed, you are. On earth, you recognize one sort of such glue by the name 'gravity.' Though invisible, odorless, and indiscriminate to the touch, the effects of gravity are discernible. Humans employ gravity to advance various ideas including those which continually expand existing technological creation.

"Our world currently incorporates a technology-that-includes-all-technology, past and present. Ever present gravity sustains all, both the old and new."

Casey: "Hmmm. Thinking about gravity as a glue that is utilized by humans as they create new technology *on earth* is a clear idea to me. I'm waiting for the bombshell. How about an idea that is just as clear when discussing new creativity *in heaven*, in your world."

Idyllica: "Throughout the All-Of-Creation, there is a barely discernible glue. Without it, relationships such as ours could not exist. Celestial order and creativity would be impossible without a binding together of some sort, a 'glue,' in terrestrial thinking."

Casey: "I can accept that."

Idyllica: "Earlier, we were reminded that the terms, 'Father' and 'Holy Spirit' help humans discuss the general nature of the All-That-Is-All. Every building block of *terrestrial* living is beget by the 'Father.' The same 'Father' is also the source of the building blocks of *celestial* living.

"The ultimate glue of creation, both terrestrial and celestial is best conveyed in the third word that is associated with the creation of All-That-Is-All. 'LOVE' is that word.

"LOVE is the ultimate attraction, the glue of All-That-Is-All. We in our celestial abode as well as you in your terrestrial environment are continuously expanding the unending experience of LOVE."

Casey: "I must interject. Having studied the conclusions of many considered among the most discerning humans to have lived on earth . . . I'm certain that you **know** them all . . . some ideas are vying for my attention at this very moment. They seem to have anticipated your clarifying the importance of a powerful, unyielding glue that holds all worlds, celestial and terrestrial, together."

Idyllica: "First, my friend, a celestial conclusion. We may refer to the experiencing of that unfathomable glue-of-creation as being 'held in His hands.' For you on the earth plane, it is a metaphorical expression. We celestials, with our continuous heavenly perception, experience the glue of LOVE unceasingly via **direct knowing**."

Casey: "I am awestruck! What has come to mind are some venerable conclusions from authors in an earlier century that address the question, then, of how a person lives a meaningful terrestrial life. I think these perspectives shed some light on our incomparable purpose *from the Creator's point-of-viewing*."

Idyllica: "We are totally in sync. I would invite you to share with your readers what you are thinking as I prepare to withdraw for the time being."

Casey: "O.K., I recall that Lucy Mallory offered this point-of-view early in the 20th century. 'A person's purpose on earth is to *be in harmony* with eternity. It is only then that the universal flow of love and intellect can be channeled through this person, as if through a clear pathway.'

"I add italic emphasis to the phrase, *be in harmony*, as I now realize that each human already lives, albeit *subconsciously*, in the now of eternity. To 'be in harmony with eternity' to me suggests an ever present *conscious* sense of **knowing** that daily, moment by

121

moment, I am engaged in the continuous expansion of love and intellect on earth."

Idyllica: "INsight-FULL! And what other conclusions regarding a life's purpose ring true with you now?"

Casey: "Leo Tolstoy observed, 'There is only one thing in this world which is worthy of dedicating all your life. This is creating more love among people and destroying barriers which exist between them.'

"In the same vein, Harriet Martineau quoted a wise man as having said, 'everyone is sent into this world with the sole purpose of loving other people.' You, my spirit friend have indicated *why* human loving is so beautifully important.

"We who love without constraint add stability to creation. We are expanding the reservoir of glue needed by the Father to bring about a peace that defies understanding, widespread peace of mind for all mankind.

"Am I making sense? Are we still in sync? Hey, where are you? Where did you go? Oops, I **know** it is not a question of *where* did you go. Rather, when will we resonate together again? *Up Is Everywhere,* right?

"Being on the same wave length is merely a matter of *when* we are being and becoming together, never a matter of some exotic spiritual place *where* we go to hook up. Right?"

No response. I feel alone.

Idyllica has gone. I **know** it. I felt a very faint tug on my heart.

—⁓⁓—

I LOVE Idyllica. I wonder if together we really are creating additional "glue" that will, somehow, lead to greater peace on earth.

Idyllica promised that *The Butterfly Revelation* truths would inevitably lead to greater peace of mind. Curiously, I do believe whole-heartedly that what the spirit of the dazzling blue butterfly has promised is absolutely *possible*.

I **know** that I am addicted to *The Butterfly Revelation*. I am fascinated by the efforts of The Caterpillar Club. And, I am more than just a bit lonely when Idyllica slips away.

I have learned so much, mostly unexpectedly. Tomorrow the adventure continues. I am beginning to wonder how long it can last. How much can I learn? I have practically filled my notebook, yet there is more to learn. I look forward to reading everything that has found its way on to the pages. I have a strong desire to acquire for myself the peace of mind that has been promised.

—⁓—

I notice a significant change in each caterpillar who is squirm-stepping toward The Caterpillar Club gathering area. Each one is getting fatter! I mean, each with a different family shape and different markings is, nevertheless, much bigger than when I first saw them. I have almost forgotten that every minute of every day when they are not under this umbrella, they are eating. You might say that the miracle of metamorphosis is "hidden in plain sight," before my very eyes.

The caterpillar seekers have arrived. It is a complete surprise to me when Woolly Bear begins today's gathering with a startling announcement.

"This is my final goodbye to all of you." Woolly's voice is resolute. The seekers are shocked. It is hard for them to imagine having any sort of group discussion without the erudite Woolly Bear providing an analytical context and an emotionally safe environment for contributions from everyone present.

"I see that you are surprised," adds Woolly Bear. "Are you so focused on *The Butterfly Revelation* scrawls that you haven't seen what is happening to us in our everyday chomp-chomp world?"

"What do you mean, Woolly?"

"I mean . . . a few of us are so bloated we can hardly wiggle-scrunch forward when we need to find a new leaf to chomp, and coming today, I stopped a half dozen times to consider, 'Is it really worth it to drag myself over there for another tidbit-tease session.'"

Monarchus IV speaks incisively, "You, friend Woolly, are obviously ready to cocoon!"

Woolly Bear swells with pride, yet, as is his new demeanor, speaks without condescension, "Yes, it appears that I am the first to begin creating a pupa. I have often wondered what I would think at this moment. Now I am living the answer. I am thinking of our grand adventure together. I am grateful for having these times of seeking and learning. Because of all of you, I *think* I am happy with my life."

There is a gentle swagging of heads. The seekers are uplifted by Woolly's words, but their bodies droop as if pulled from within by heavy hearts.

Woolly is continuing, "I did not anticipate the feeling that would accompany this moment. Even as I look into the faces of my dearest friends, I confess, I *feel* lonely. Do you wonder why I am feeling lonely?" There is a long pause.

Woolly, the master of logic and exposition continues a bit softer. "I can explain. I feel somewhat alone because I realize that cocooning is something I must do all by myself. So, even though I am among friends for the moment, I am feeling the loneliness that is to begin perhaps only moments after we say 'goodbyes' to each other."

Woolly's sense of impending loneliness does not arouse empathy with everyone. "Are we not going to consider a fragment today?" is a question raised by one of the more practical seekers.

Woolly Bear is ready for the question. "I think you all should definitely carry on and consider a new *Revelation* scrawl. I suggest that Monarchus lead the contemplation today. And now, if you will excuse me."

"Gladly, great explorer of life's secrets," Monarchus IV is generous. "Your zest for unlocking mysteries inspired us. We will be faithful to that spirit today. Go proudly. Build a superb cocoon."

Woolly Bear moves away slowly. He turns and scans the steadfast seekers. His voice is strong, full of assurance.

"Farewell, my dear and loyal friends. Please know that after yesterday's INsight I am convinced that I will be constructing a gateway. I am at peace. I expect to live!"

—◦◦◦—

Woolly Bear, the one time egocentric seeker of plaudits for his pithy remarks, is utterly sincere. He is simply stating the truth as he perceives it for himself. He is not trying to persuade others and he is no longer concerned about his reputation. As for living a purpose-filled life, Woolly seems explicitly to *be in harmony* with eternity.

Woolly Bear's pomposity has dwindled away. His aggrandizing attitude has totally disappeared. Woolly's life, indeed, has expanded intellect and love on earth. Woolly, I would argue, is in harmony with life, with GOD.

Exhibiting true harmony, all the caterpillars begin cheering, applauding and wiggle-waving "goodbye" to their confident fuzzy friend. The fading noise of a loving farewell is the last sound Woolly Bear ever hears . . . as a caterpillar.

The seekers turn their attention to Monarchus IV. Pixie speaks for everyone, "We need for you, My Dear, to lead us from this time on." It is the first time that Pixie, publicly, has shown her affection for her beloved Monarchus IV. She lowers her head to mask the sudden blush of embarrassment. She didn't really mean to say, "My Dear," out loud.

Monarchus IV actually heard the difference in Pixie's voice for the first time. He always enjoys her presence and long has been impressed that she seems to be the one seeker who is as passionate about unlocking the *Revelation* secrets as he himself. What he has missed is the love!

Pixie's passion is not primarily about the ancient wisdom. Pixie's passion has always been to be near Monarchus IV. Monarchus IV is tempted to engage Pixie in a conversation to determine what exactly did she mean when she said, "My Dear," where everyone could hear. The moment escapes.

Monarchus IV lets the fleeting "love flutter" get away as he concentrates on the expectant faces of the seekers. They want today's scrawl. Monarchus IV obliges. He shuffles to the stack of remaining leaf fragments and draws the top leaf toward the center of the "wisdom ring" as it was once described by Woolly Bear, their now departed "ringmaster."

All Life Moments Ripple Interminably

Monarchus IV has never seen nor heard the word, interminably, in his home or in his time at school. He pronounces the word syllable by syllable.

"IN´-ter-min-AB´-ly." He hesitatingly tries again, "Inter-MIN´-a-BLEE´."

He is stumbling, struggling, floundering, so unMonarchus-like. The other gatherers are bewildered. No one is moving. No one is speaking.

Pixie is feeling Monarchus's fluster. She breaks the group's icy mental paralysis with an upbeat suggestion.

"I have an idea." Pixie is always sparkly and the others move their attention from Monarchus IV to the delightful Pixie.

"Let's celebrate today, our final day with Woolly Bear, by taking a break from *The Butterfly Revelation* and by crooning our newest chorus in his honor." Within seconds the entire huddled assembly is swaying and singing.

Trust The Cocoon, ooh-ooh-aye-aye
gateway, gateway, to the sky-aye.

Over and over, the robust chorus creates an indelible memory. *Ooh-ooh-aye-aye . . . to the sky-aye.* After a time, they poop out.

The seekers have interrupted their contemplation of ancient wisdom. The newest scrawl is abandoned. Awhile later, the still humming caterpillars wobble-nod "goodbye" to each other. Slowly, the distracted seekers are retreating. A pall is in the sir.

Woolly Bear is gone. There is something quite somber about the scene I am witnessing. The mood is solemn like that which invariably hovers over a group of glum mourners leaving a cemetery. Something special has ended and there is nothing more to say.

Monarchus IV is befuddled by the newly considered *Revelation* INsight. He alone is still thinking about the five-word scrawl. Pixie is reluctant to leave his side yet her concentration is dissipating. She, too, is feeling an inexplicable urge to go. I sense that her rising inclination is similar to that of Woolly Bear's just before his clear decision to get on with his cocooning.

I am focused on the mind energy of the departing Caterpillar Club gatherers and, for once, I am receiving absolutely nothing. It is as if no one is thinking at all about today's gathering. I am picking up vague shadows only. I suspect them to be cocoon-like images.

The silent shadowy images are now rapidly fading. As the caterpillars move farther away, I am losing my connection. I have lost contact. All but two of the caterpillar gatherers are gone.

I watch with lingering fascination as Pixie and Monarchus IV also begin moving away from the wisdom ring. Both seem disappointed that they are giving up on the scrawl of the day. Simultaneously, with similarly dejected looks, they briefly turn their heads toward the leafy fragment. Intuitively, each turns away and unswervingly creeps out of the circle . . . in opposite directions!

How was I to know today was the final meeting . . . EVER! . . . of my Caterpillar Club? The Being & Becoming Bunch, as they identified themselves, never gathered again. Indeed, on the same day that Woolly Bear left the group, Monarchus IV stopped eating and began searching for an ideal location to form his own cocoon.

Just across an open patch of matted grass Monarchus IV spied a green leaf luxuriant milkweed plant. I last saw him headed in that direction, seemingly preoccupied, in plain view of potential predators.

I do not want to leave. I am absorbed completely in my own thoughts. I have been contemplating the scrawled INsight, *All Life Moments Ripple Interminably*, and cannot help wondering if I will ever unravel its meaning. I have been drifting, drowsy, disconnected from time itself. I do not have any idea how long I have been in this state-of-mind.

VI
SIR CHARLES MANTIS, ILC*
Happiness: A Mantis Point-Of-View

Wait! Something unexpected, totally unexpected, is happening. I sense a new, completely unknown presence. Clearly, it is an insect of some kind. I am familiar with many of the insect languages. However, it is unprecedented for me to be contacted when I'm engrossed in my own thoughts.

An Unknown Presence (haughty, crass, condescending): "Well, well, well. What have we here? The Bug Guy! Finally, we meet."

Casey (confused, searching, subdued): "What? . . . Where? . . . Who? . . ."

Unknown Presence: "Look *into* the greenery, not under it. At first, you will not notice me. You see only green leaves and skinny, brown branches. However, Bug Guy, I'm here nearly every day watching and listening to these utterly foolish caterpillars. So amusing, so dopey!"

Casey: "Please. Identify yourself. I AM peering *into* the leaves. Oh, there, I see you now."

Unknown Presence: "At your service, Sir Charles Mantis, Crown Prince of the grand Mantis clan. You may call me 'Charlie' as I am known to my friends. Proudly, I am known as 'Chucklin' Charlie' to my prey."

*ILC = Insect Life Coach
ILC Mantra: Eat Well Today. Tomorrow We Die.

Casey: "The Mantis Clan? I have never communicated with a mantis, Charlie. You say that you have been here almost every day?"

Charlie Mantis: "Oh yeah. But it's not my style to stick my head out to be seen by all the bugs, beetles and nerd caterpillars in the world. I look at them the way you look at a restaurant menu. The difference is that I must catch my lunch by preying. You pray and someone brings you your lunch."

Casey: "You have been preying upon the caterpillars who meet here?"

Charlie Mantis: "Ah, Bug Guy, what a genius you are. Preying is what I do! So, of course, I had the caterpillar fools in my sight. I have been watching them get fatter and fatter. But, oh my goodness, what nonsense I have had to withstand to get close to them."

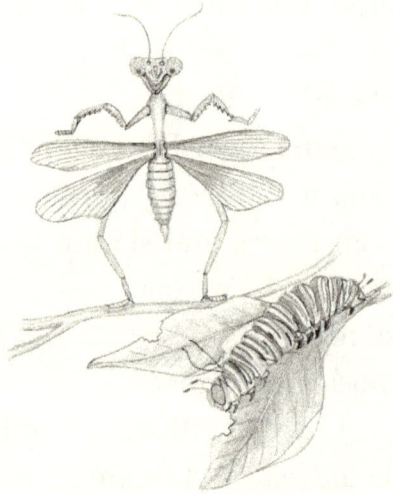

Casey: "Nonsense? What do you mean by nonsense?"

Charlie Mantis: "C'mon, Bug Guy, you must know the crazy stuff these poor pollyannas talk about. When they should be helping their families do their designated leaf chomping, these airheads are jabbering about transforming themselves in some unthinkable, unknowable, unbelievable, uncreepable way. Pure nonsense. And, get this . . . they are serious! To them, it is no joke. To me, it is hilarious."

Casey: "I do not think they are airheads at all. Trying to understand transformation and transcendence is an honorable, levelheaded, almost sacred thing to do. In the human world such activity is thought to be enlightening. It is called seeking wisdom. What do you call it?"

Charlie Mantis: "To be honest, talk of transforming and transcending is gobbledegook."

Casey: "Really and truly? You call the desire to know about the future 'gobbledegook'?"

Charlie Mantis: "We mantis live for today. You want to live? Find good stuff to eat. You want to live forever? Keep on finding good stuff to eat. You want to know about the future? Learn where to find a good meal today. The future will take care of itself. That is the Mantis way."

Casey: "That's it? You don't care what is going to happen to you and all the Mantis clan? You're satisfied to think that when you can no longer capture a meal for yourself, you just lie down and die?"

Charlie Mantis: "There IS nothing beyond dying. There is no Big-Mantis-In-The-Sky, if that is what you are wondering. Happiness is a great meal and stimulating conversation about the here-and-now. In fact, I'm very happy to finally have made your acquaintance. What's up with you?"

Casey: "Hold on a minute. I want to be sure I understand you. Having a great meal today is your idea of living a fulfilled life? A meal satisfies you?"

Charlie Mantis: "Amen. 'You can take that to the bank' is the way I think humans express it."

Casey: "Perhaps I can learn more about your point-of-view? You certainly have a way of thinking that is different from that of the caterpillar friends that I have been observing."

Charlie Mantis: "I am happy to summarize for you. There is no better meal than a plump Monarch larvae, maybe two. Earlier today, not all that long ago, I was preying to find such a delectable treat. Finding such makes life worth living today and every day."

Casey: "You live only for today. You seek pleasure now. You pooh-pooh the caterpillars' desire to understand a possible transformation that could follow a lifetime of eating and struggling to avoid being eaten. Am I correct? Is this your outlook?"

Charlie Mantis: "Yes. 'On the money' is the phrase you might use. [chucklin'] Listen up, I'll tell you the difference between the Monarch family and the Mantis family. The Monarchs do the chomping, we Mantis do the preying. I'll grant you they work hard. We, on the other hand, work smart." [Again, Charlie is chucklin' as if he has said something very profound.]

Casey: "So, you reject all caterpillar ideas of transformation or transcendence?"

Charlie Mantis: (sneering tone) "Listen, Bug Guy. Monarch clan wise guys have farfetched notions about transforming themselves.

"We know better. We eat them. You might say we recycle Monarchs. How's that for transformation?"

Casey: "Honestly, Charlie, yours is an appalling life view. I wonder if you or the Mantis generations to follow will ever explore the possibility that life does not end when preying for meals ends?"

Charlie Mantis: [sighing] "Well, Bug Guy, we won't speculate on that today. I have just finished the most scrumptious meal of my young life. I am not sure you want to hear about it."

Casey: "No, that's all right. Go ahead. I'm curious about everything insects do."

Charlie Mantis: "Well, I came upon a Monarch that was so stuffed it could hardly wiggle, much less waggle. It took all my strength to lift the creeper with my pincers and hold it steady while I devoured the flesh and drank the ooze. Succulent, succulent, succulent. And now, I am really ready for a nap."

Casey: "Sickening. I am ready for a mind cleansing, really ready!"

Charlie Mantis: "So long, Bug Guy. I'm outta here. Gotta find a comfortable place to digest today's happiness!"

———

I fear that Charlie's victim was Monarchus IV. I truly am sickened to think the death of a friend brings sheer happiness to anyone, much less a smug predator.

And that is how I learned that a great misfortune befell Monarchus IV. Full details are unknown to me but there is much I can assume. In his chubby state Monarchus IV moved so slowly that he was defenseless when he was unexpectedly confronted by an old family nemesis, Chucklin' Charlie Mantis.

To his great delight, Chucklin' Charlie observed Monarchus IV as he departed the very last Caterpillar Club gathering. Monarchus IV was moving very sluggishly across the open grassy space. Charlie was hungry, voraciously hungry. On another occasion he might have ignored a caterpillar so large and swollen. Not today.

Monarchus IV did not have a chance to survive. His final conscious caterpillar moments were spent dangling helplessly from the pair of mantis pincers whose possessor Monarchus IV had not seen nor anticipated. I am saddened as I report. Monarchus IV will never fly. In fact, he never even began constructing his cocoon.

I have lost contact with Sir Charles Mantis. He is sleeping, digesting, dormant, cut off from me and I welcome the distance.

I am despondent to tell the truth. I realize that entering another's life vicariously can be an emotional experience. But *experiencing* another's life as it is being lived, as I had with Monarchus IV and his friends, is deeper. The closest word I know is "empathy," to actually understand and to share another's feelings.

To *live* another's happiness and despair is **knowing** another. With Monarchus IV gone, something of mySELF is missing. That something is with him! What is it? Where does it go? Is such a loss retrievable?

I long to be with Monarchus IV, Woolly Bear, Pixie, and the others. I want again to be completely engaged in the struggle to unlock the most recent *Revelation* scrawl.

My heart, mind and soul are agonizing in concert.
I pine as one who is completely absorbed in the loss of
a loved one. I am empty of all words. They are
insufficient. Words cannot substitute for love lost. I
can remember the scene, the final caterpillar
gathering, as if it were just a few minutes ago. Yet I
cannot *remember* the love. Our love was unseen,
unheard, untouched. It was *lived*! Now, in its place, a
hollowness.

VII
THE HEREAFTER
A Different Point-Of-Viewing

I had been so concentrating on Woolly Bear's departure, Pixie's embarrassment, and Monarchus IV's vocabulary challenge that I hadn't given the content of today's *Revelation* INsight a second thought. From the moment Pixie diverted the group's attention from the leaf fragment to an uplifting celebration croon highlighting Woolly's decision to begin cocooning, I had been locked onto the here-and-now of the caterpillar club break-up. Of course, Sir Charles Mantis interrupted everything.

I am startled by a sudden infiltration. I am receiving a mind encompassing "Hello" from the spirit that I **know** as Idyllica. The intensity of my heart's longing to love and my mind's longing to **know** has apparently opened my consciousness to the spirit of the dazzling blue butterfly.

Idyllica's thoughts give no hint that time has passed, that a caterpillar club break-up has occurred, or a guzzling mantis has cracked my heart.

Casey: "Hello?!? Wow! Hello yourself!"

Idyllica: "What are your impressions of today's gathering?"

Casey: "I am reeling a bit. Have you ever witnessed such a surprising change? Never had it occurred to me that *real cocooning* might actually interfere with the *study of cocooning*. When the cocoon urge strikes, it is 'goodbye ancient wisdom,' isn't it? That was totally unexpected. Wow, what a change!"

Idyllica: "During my caterpillar phase, I was given a maxim that covers such a time as we witnessed today. 'If you expect change, it will not be unexpected.' You humans have many similar statements. A most common cliché, I suppose, is that which says, 'The only thing permanent is change.'

"I believe you have a special label for expressions such as 'permanent change.' You call them 'oxymorons,' do you not?"

Casey: "Oh yes, we have innumerable contradictions in our lives and in our minds. When they are so outrageous, we do call them 'oxymorons,' indeed."

Idyllica: "I have learned that among humans much misunderstanding, confusion and limitation is simply a disconnect between experience and language. We *know* what we experience even when we can't decide what words to use in telling others about the experience. Occasionally, what is communicated is the opposite of what was meant. I suppose we could call that an 'oxymoronic exchange,' eh?"

Casey: "Yes, we could. Also, there are many self-contradictory statements which we call 'paradoxes.' Telling someone that we must experience death in order to live would be such a paradox and, upon first hearing or reading that idea, one might quickly determine that it was stupid, or 'jabberwock' to quote a best loved story about a girl in a mythical Wonderland."

Idyllica: "To be certain I understand, give me an example of this dying-and-living paradox, if you would please."

Casey: "Alright. Even though you, Idyllica, have died a natural butterfly death, you are most certainly alive in this moment. That, to most readers, would be paradoxical. To some, incomprehensible."

Idyllica: "Well, words may clarify and words may confuse. The best alternative is mutual experience. Even then, the meaning of an experience and its effect will be different for any two individuals regardless of how similar they may appear to be."

Casey: "This is why *The Butterfly Revelation* messages will mean different things to different people regardless of the explanations that you have given me. For me, the goal is to be as clear as I can be about what I am learning. I have no desire to convince others that what I am learning is the *only* possible learning.

"In fact, I have no desire to convince others that what I am learning is truer or better than what anyone else might learn from the same or similar experiences. I just trust that the words you are giving me are the best we might have chosen."

Idyllica: "They are. Today, however, we have the ultimate wisdom thought to unravel. The entire crux of everything that is **known** or **knowable** is wrapped up in just five words, one of which, I suspect, you have never used correctly in any conversation. It is clear that Monarchus IV and your special caterpillar seeker friends had never encountered the word at all."

Casey: "Ah, words, words, words. We seem to have no choice. We are limited to words. Is communicating with words really going to be a problem we cannot overcome?"

Idyllica: "Overcome the limitation? No. Minimize the problem? Yes. We reduce misunderstanding, never eliminate it. Here's why.

"Written words present the straightforward dilemma that the meaning of a specific word is perceived differently by various readers and, even with agreement among several readers, the discerned meaning may be somewhat different from what the writer intended. Spoken words may be equally misunderstood because the meaning is obscured by demeanor, inflection and gestures, as well as colloquial patterns."

Casey: "Let's give it our best shot!"

Idyllica: "We shall! Ready to go?"

Casey: "I'm pumped! But, are you really saying that today's *Butterfly Revelation* scrawl, this single ancient INsight, really is much more comprehensive than the others? I cannot imagine that to be accurate."

Idyllica: "Trust me on this one."

Casey: "And, really and truly, how can one word that I don't ever use correctly be the one word that is critical?"

Idyllica: "Keep your mind open. We need to go deep, deeper than most humans care to contemplate. Among humans, ideas about death remain surprisingly shallow because ideas about life have barely scratched the surface of its true essence.

141

"We are about to resonate deeply with the *Pulse Of The Revelation,* what the ancient INsight reveals about all life that has ever existed, all life that is existing, and all life that shall ever exist."

Casey: "Speaking of all life, before, here, and hereafter, does not seem like a particularly deep starting place. These are all simple words with which I am familiar. Am I missing something?"

Idyllica: "Not yet."

Casey: "Today's scrawl has five words, *All Life Moments Ripple Interminably.* Could you ease my mind along one word at a time?"

Idyllica: "Certainly. That IS a reasonable approach. and I know you are most comfortable taking things slowly. That will be true for most of your readers as well.

"There will be readers, of course, who prefer to jump right to the finish line without feeling the strain of the race and the ardor of the breakthrough which occurs when one has put every ounce of being into a long running event and prevailed. High jumpers, I suppose."

Casey: "Yes, and you do **know**, I am not the 'high jumper' type. I am really wholeheartedly ready for the entire race. Let's go!"

Idyllica: "Ready. Take your mark. Get set. And we will slowly GO. Our starting line, then, is a simple word, *All.* Would you accept 'nothing left out or overlooked' as a fair use of 'all'? 'Nothing *of any kind* left out' is important to accept."

Casey: "I am comfortable with the idea that the INsight, whatever its subject, means to include every bit of that subject matter. There is to be no exception, nothing beyond, nothing excluded."

Idyllica: "Good. We continue to a complex word, *Life*. While the typical use of the word is limited to those things which grow and reproduce, including humans, I am going to suggest a bit more inclusive word, *Existence*. I want you to consider that the scrawl is about *everything known to exist*, whether it is described as 'animate' or 'inanimate,' or described as 'living' or 'dead,' in your earthbound language.

"Is such a meaning O.K. with you?"

Casey: "I am incapable of comprehending a concept such as 'all existence,' but the general use of the two words is fine. I think I would say that I can *know about* such an idea even if I cannot fully **know** that to which the words apply."

Idyllica: "That is good enough. The next word on the leaf, *Moments*, is not restricted to earth time thinking. You are used to thinking about time in earth durations, that is, years, days, hours, minutes, and seconds. Such terms are all used in reference to the earth, which is your home, and one star in the cosmos which you call 'the sun.' These are definable aspects of earth time *only*.

"Today's INsight, however, is about *All Existence*, and in that realm, *Moments* is a timeless designation. Earthlings use the word 'moment' in an attempt to sort out when or where an event may have occurred from an earth time perspective.

"Consider this idea. *All Existence* experiences *All Moments* simultaneously and continuously, 'now' and 'eternally' for they are the same."

Casey: "Ooooh, I think we just went a little deeper into the meaning of this scrawl."

Idyllica: "Good for you. We are going deeper but we are not going to get lost or disappear. We are not going to be left out or overlooked in the realm of existence.

"On the contrary, we, you and I in spirit concert, are creating a moment which is absolutely unique having never been created ever before in just this particular way. We are involved in the creation of creation. We are helping to create both a terrestrial and celestial future . . . right now!"

Casey: "So, every moment is unique having never existed before whether in 'earth time' or in 'existence time.' Is that a correct way to understand?"

Idyllica: "Quite correctly understood. The next word, *Ripple*, takes us even deeper. This word is the most easily understood by humans; however, in this thought bundle, its implications are far reaching."

Casey: "Yes, ripple is one word that I think I understand well. When I see or hear the word ripple, I always think of the same image."

Idyllica: "Yes, I am aware of that image as it is in your mind at this time. For future readers of these notes, why don't you go ahead and write what you are seeing."

Casey: "I see a pond. A pebble has been dropped into the pond. What I see are small concentric circles of waves, the ripples, moving evenly in all directions from the spot where the pebble entered the water. The ripples look like rings on the surface of the pond. The rings, or waves, move steadily toward the shoreline around the pond. When they arrive at the pond's edge they sort of slap-slap on the shore then retreat and disappear. The pond, once again, is glassy calm."

Idyllica: "Lovely. After my transformation from creeper to flyer, I discovered ponds. Flying above a beautiful blue pond was a favorite early morning activity. I 'see' a rippling pond now."

Casey: "WE 'see' it now!"

Idyllica: "Yes, it is in OUR minds' eyes."

Casey: "I'll include an image for readers of my notebook."

Idyllica: "As you are aware, that was my thought, too."

Casey: "What about the INsight? Let's get back to that. What would you have me consider?"

Idyllica: "Could you accept that, in your mind's eye pond, a ripple *could be caused* by a leaf blown from an overhanging tree branch?"

Casey: "I've never thought of that, but I am sure a very slight ripple might be caused by a falling leaf."

Idyllica: "Could you accept that, in your mind's eye pond, a ripple *could be caused* by a feather floating gently down from the body of a goose flying through a rigorous headwind high over the pond?"

Casey: "I can accept the idea, but it sure wouldn't be much of a ripple, would it?"

Idyllica: "Oh, quite the contrary, it would create a significant ripple. Bugs that scurry on the pond's surface, as well as nearly invisible organisms that huddle on the underside of the pond's surface, would immediately be aware that their universe had been disturbed by a huge, unknown intruder."

Casey: "Aha! You sneaked the old point-of-viewing INsight perspective into my mind. Whether or not there is a significant ripple on the pond does not depend upon a human opinion. Rather, the ripple's nature and significance depends upon who or what you are and where you are when you experience such a real disturbance of the pond's surface. I shall keep that in mind. Apparently, I will need that perspective to go deeper into this thought."

Idyllica: "You are quick and correct to identify the important shift of attention that understanding this INsight will require. Let me ask further, could you accept that in your mind's eye pond, a ripple *could be caused* by a moonbeam? And, you do know that the moon itself doesn't cast a light beam toward the earth? The so-called 'moonbeam' is simply sunlight reflected from an object that would otherwise be completely dark, unseen by the human eye."

Casey: "Moonbeams causing ripples in ponds on earth? Honestly? That would not occur to me. In fact, this is an even tougher notion to accept than the goose feather ripple. My first reaction, as I'm sure you already know, is you'd need to prove it to me."

Idyllica: "Sorry. Today, I am not in the proving business. I am, more or less, teaching in the mind-opening school. And, I must say that up until now you have been an excellent student."

Casey: "Thank you. That is encouraging. At times I feel like the class dunce."

Idyllica: "One final probe. Could you accept that in your mind's eye pond, a ripple *could be caused* by a thought originating *in the mind* of the person tossing the pebble into the water?"

Casey: "Oh my, no. That is too far out. Pardon me, but to think that a human thought could cause a pond to ripple is a preposterous idea."

Idyllica: "Hang on. Thankfully, you did not say 'impossible.' That word, I must warn you, will shut off your mind. We need your mind to be open because we are going still deeper."

Casey: "Don't worry. I am not going to shut down. I was merely giving my first reaction."

Idyllica: "Well, let's find out what else you would be willing to consider. Would you accept that the ripple caused by the tossed stone may have created wrinkles that traveled to the bottom of the pond and not just across the surface?"

Casey: "I simply do not know if that can happen. I do not reject the idea. Yet, to be honest, I cannot accept something so quickly that I have never thought about before."

Idyllica: "Your reluctance to form hasty conclusions or to accept ideas without adequate reflection are traits that will help your readers. Each of them, too, will be faced with embracing or discarding the ideas conveyed by *The Butterfly Revelation*. Readers will appreciate that you are taking time to assimilate what you are receiving."

Casey: "Thank you. Now, where are we?"

Idyllica: "For an additional moment, we will focus on the pond in your mind. You aren't as sure about a ripple that moves into and through the pond as you are about a ripple that appears to move upon the pond's surface. That is fine. At this point, certainty isn't nearly as important as *possibility*. Now, I have one final pond question for you to consider."

Casey: "I am ready."

Idyllica: "Thinking about the pond in your mind, where do the ripples end?"

Casey: "Easy answer. Each ripple, in its turn, ends at the shoreline."

Idyllica: "That is the obvious terrestrial answer. It is a human-on-the-shore answer. It is a caterpillar answer. Indeed, it is also a butterfly answer. However, it is NOT the correct answer. Your answer is a limiting answer. Such an answer will prevent your absorbing the true meaning of the scrawl we are unraveling."

Casey: "I do not want to fall short, to be limited, as you call it. I want to understand. More than that, I want the peace of mind that you claim is the natural legacy bestowed on anyone who understands the full message of *The Butterfly Revelation*."

Idyllica: "Then you are ready to entertain an expanded idea of ripple. You are ready to leave the pond where, from your point-of-viewing, each ripple ends at the shoreline."

Casey: "A ripple does not end at the shoreline? I'm sorry. I say it does. That, indeed, IS my point-of-view."

Idyllica: "And, I would insist that ripple is an action that, once begun, *does not ever end*. In this particular scrawl, *Ripple* is a word that describes an *omni*directional phenomenon that will approach, but never quite reach, the very edge of *Existence* itself."

Casey: "I sense fog beginning to obscure my thinking. What is my problem?"

Idyllica: "My friend, you have no problem. You are simply being drawn away from your concrete earth understanding about ponds, pebbles and ripples. This idea is deep, very deep. The ancients perceived that every movement, thought, feeling and breath experienced on the earth creates a ripple *throughout the full expanse of creation*."

Casey: "I am breathless. I am beyond deep. I am mind saturated."

Idyllica: "You are not at all saturated, my partner. Rather, you are totally alive . . . body, mind, heart and spirit.

"You are nearer than ever to **knowing** the peace of mind that accompanies a full understanding of the *Revelation*. I shall now withdraw briefly so that you might unhurriedly absorb a few nuances of the simple truth that *All Life Moments Ripple* . . ."

[The moments that passed at this point may have been few or many. I have no way of knowing.]

Casey: (musing) "So, a ripple occurs when a substance (e.g., water, sand) is disturbed in some way (e.g., pebble splashing, wind blowing) and the result is an undulation or wave being set in motion. If you followed the ripple or wave pattern backward, you would be able to determine where is started. Some ripples are indiscernible to the naked eye and some, apparently, are incapable of detection even using the subatomic microscopic tools available to modern man.

"The shapes and paths of all the ripples that have ever been created, never go away! That means a record of all the lives and conditions that have ever existed on earth is present now within the **knowable** creation that is itself ongoing.

"For humans who invoke their natural celestial nature, all creation, before, after, here, there, and hereafter, is available for exploration and enjoyment! *Ripples* record all existence?!?

"The meaning of the idea itself that I am trying to grasp is NOT foggy. Quite the contrary is true. The meaning is simple and clear. What is problematic is whether it is *conceivably* true. Can my mind wrap itself around the implications of an idea that, to me, is so revolutionary? Further, does it even matter what I think?"

150

There is a sudden rush of energy that feels strangely like a time recently when I laughed so hard I almost cried. I don't think you would say I am suddenly filled with happiness. I think it is more than that. I suddenly feel exhilarated. Idyllica is equally buoyant. Our feelings mesh!

Idyllica: "You have been doing some heavy pondering. I am pleased that you clearly grasp the idea this *Revelation* beacon is conveying. Creation records and maintains a cosmic vault containing a record of all 'new moments' that have ever occurred and are occurring now. The ancients simply referred to this phenomenon as *All Life Moments Ripple* . . ."

Casey: "Yes, some say 'akasha' (from the Sanscrit word, *ākāśa)* to refer to the same phenomenon."

Idyllica: "What you may not yet have tried to understand is the truth about ripples that lies beyond what most of your fellow humans are willing to imagine. You need a runner's second wind for a breakthrough."

Casey: "That sounds somewhat mystifying. To what are you referring?"

Idyllica: "Let's try out the idea of a ripple that never abates. It is an idea that one of your favorites, the teacher who called himself 'the son of man,' offered to his surrogate teachers. 'Not one bird falls from the sky' without its being noted by the Father, the all-inclusive spirit for which some use the word, God. The teacher added that not 'one hair on the head' is ever lost. Each hair leaves its trail, its record, in the archives of creation to which you and I have access. Is that idea acceptable or mystifying to you at this time?"

151

Casey: "Both. I do accept the idea, but I am completely mystified that this record takes place at all times continuously, including all peoples, locations and events on the earth. I mean, this seems crazy! There is a permanently recorded archive of A SINGLE HAIR? ALL HAIRS?!?"

Idyllica: "Ah, unabated ripples even include a ripple that is created by the flapping of a butterfly's wing, by the slither of a worm's torso, by the exhaling of your breath, and even by the thoughts that we are generating at this very instant. What do you think of that?"

Casey : "You already know that as much as I want to accept the truth that all manifestations of life create ripples, I cannot get my mind around such a possibility."

Idyllica: "Great! You used the word 'possibility' and that allows you to go with me even deeper along with the ancients who authored *The Butterfly Revelation*."

Casey: "Even deeper? How is it possible to go deeper?"

Idyllica: "Simple. Just finish the thought. Ponder the entire declaration. Tackle the word that you have never used in your life. Give your complete heart and mind over to the possibility that not only does every new occurrence in all of creation add an indelible trace to the fundamental fabric of existence, but also open your heart and mind to embrace that these traces, these ripples themselves, exist *interminably*."

Casey: "Interminably, interminably, interminably…"

Idyllica: "Yes. Without end."

Casey: "The scrawl says that everything that has ever happened everywhere has created a ripple, an identifiable record. Such records of *everything that has ever happened* may change form but are accessible to the mind and will never be destroyed. Am I close to the meaning found on the leaf fragment?"

Idyllica: "That, indeed, is the gist of the fragment. This INsight, more than any other, hints at the utter excitement, joy and fulfillment of the celestial life that awaits you after your transcendence."

Casey: "Explain that, if you would."

Idyllica: "You know how limited you are in *physically* experiencing all that one human could experience while living on the earth. Should you begin today to experience for yourself the wonders of every continent, the miracles in every ocean, the amazements within the microscopic world, the incredulities of every telescopic galactic discovery, no number of 24-hour earth days would be enough for you to complete your exploration.

"Should you live to be a million *physically constrained* years old, you still couldn't come close to experiencing all that has evolved within the terrestrial vibe on your home planet, within your home solar system and throughout your current galactic environment. And, you know that your scientists have recently discovered millions of galaxies in just one small previously dark corner of space. 'Worlds without end' is a description used by those on the cutting edge of your space sciences."

Casey: "Yes, I myself have long been fascinated that humans who lived on earth before the cataclysmic planet wide flood some 10,000 years ago knew much more about other planets, other stars, and other galaxies than perhaps we have yet to know. Some of the inexplicable structures, cultural traditions, archaeological anomalies, obscure written and oral accounts that have been revealed to increasing numbers of curious human seekers excite me and give me moments of 'aha' similar to that of a detective who resolves the cause of a mysterious circumstance.

"I realize that I cannot learn all that I want to learn about things that I actually have seen and heard, much less untold phenomena about which I have never seen nor heard. I just assume that I have one life to live. Whatever I learn, I learn. About everything else, I suppose I will remain ignorant."

Idyllica: "No, no, my friend, you will not remain ignorant. Because of creation's ripples, upon realizing your transcendent celestial capabilities, your curiosity need know no limitation."

Casey: "No limitation?"

Idyllica: "No limitation."

Casey: "This may seem weird, but what if I am curious about persons who lived hundreds or even thousands of years ago? Can I meet them? Will I recognize them? I mean, if I and others who have lived on earth before are simply to become 'light energy beings' of some sort, I can only imagine the hereafter to be a hodgepodge of sparkling, rainbow, dazzling luminescences everywhere. I no doubt need imagination alteration."

Idyllica: "No, you need answers to your questions. Allow me.

"You will have infinite access to all lives, here and hereafter. You will be as intimately aware of each personality whom you desire to **know** as each of them will be aware of you. Further, if you are so inclined, you may engage the ripples of another time and space and **know** the full unfolding of a particular soul, a group of souls, or an environment devoid of human souls altogether."

Casey: "How can that be?"

Idyllica: "You will be clothed in a new garment, or dwelling, whose capabilities to transcend time, space, matter and humanity are as incomprehensible to you at this moment as flying was incomprehensible to me during my earth experience as a caterpillar. Are you with me?"

Casey: "I'm awed. I'm astonished. I am wonderFILLED! I had never imagined the Kingdom Of Heaven to be so marvelous. 'Going to heaven' actually means 'becoming heavenly,' doesn't it?"

Idyllica: "Yes. I **know** you have not ever allowed your mind to soar spiritually as it might. Regrettably, you have restricted your understanding by repeated ritualistic incantations and images of heaven being likened to a 'new city with golden streets and pearly gates.' No image could be more terrestrial, more earth like, more concrete than that of a city.

"To further ensnarl your spiritual soaring capacity, you have over and over again allowed the word 'worship' to inform your mind that living in an heavenly vibration would somehow involve incessant

155

singing, saluting, and salaaming to a figure draped in a glowing white garment.

"Granted, His garment is said to be priceless and 'not made with human hands.' But frankly, this ONE to be worshipped, in countless paintings, sketches and dramas, looks awfully similar to a character actor wearing a bathrobe."

Casey: "I am laughing about an actor wearing a bathrobe and can barely relate to what you just communicated."

Idyllica: "Yes, you are chortling . . . unfortunately! You, and other millions have intellectually created a heaven in your mind which is like earth. Such self-oriented, sorry speculating is a peace-busting life tragedy."

Casey: "Tragedy?"

Idyllica: "Yes. The great teachers have always taught that heaven with all its glorious manifestations is overwhelmingly experienced as LOVE. Thus, *the higher teaching has always been that earth ought to be a reflection of heaven, not the other way around*.

"The old actor in a bathrobe to whom humans intellectually genuflect is, unfortunately, brought out for display on certain days, in certain places, and during certain ritualistic acts described as worship. Heaven, and The Old Man are thought to be far away, somewhere beyond the blue.

"Meanwhile, LOVE, The Holy Spirit, struggles on earth to overcome its nemesis, human lives devoid of God-loving neighbors who every day love *all others* as they love themselves.

"LOVE is to be *lived with your neighbors*. Indeed, LOVE is always *at hand*. Too often, however, the love-word is hijacked for parading and proselytizing. It is a great unfortunate tragedy."

Casey: "I am realizing a brazen new interpretation of the thought pattern, 'Thy kingdom come, Thy will be done, on earth as it is in heaven.' You describe the ultimate impression one experiences in the celestial, or heavenly, mode as being enveloped by LOVE.

"For life to be 'on earth as it is in heaven,' LOVE, not just the love-word must permeate every situation. Am I correct?"

Idyllica: "Yes, that's it, indeed. You are enjoying a detective moment. You are deep, deep, deep into *The Butterfly Revelation*, and you are discovering simple truths and understanding them correctly."

Casey: "I am still foggy about God, or 'Our Father, who art in heaven.' I need help."

Idyllica: "God, as your earlier notes concluded, is a controversial *word*, nothing more, nothing less. You recall the conclusion that heaven describes *what you become, not where you go*. Together, we concluded, that **direct knowing** is an acceptable way to acknowledge when an individual is experiencing 'heaven on earth.' I would propose that if love is undetectable in any situation on earth, then, while God, indeed, is present, the *Glory Of God* is, at that moment, subservient to the perplexity of men and women."

Casey: "You cannot get fresh water and salt water from the tap at the same time!"

Idyllica: "I admire the elegance of such a teaching, and the purity of a teacher such as the one whom you are quoting. The images, parables, metaphors and acts of men and women fully expressing the Holy Spirit of LOVE, the glue of the Kingdom Of Heaven, are like beacons demonstrating how to *love* daily 'on earth as it is in heaven.'

"Truly wise men and women of every age continue to pass along abiding wisdom from those spiritual avatars who came before. The way to experience 'heaven' is available to all who are unquenchably curious and persistently seeking INsight."

Casey: "Who are the wise men and women of *this* age?"

Idyllica: "You, my friend, are becoming one of the wise ones of your time. Believe me, the wisdom you are seeking and discerning will be like a beacon on a hill to countless others."

Casey: "By sharing *The Butterfly Revelation* I am a beacon of love? Hunh uh. I don't think so."

Idyllica: "You have forgotten momentarily what together we set out to do when we first became consciously interwoven. Granted, we didn't use the imagery of a beacon on a hill. However, we did define clearly what we believed would be the grandest gift we could offer men and women."

Casey: "Please refresh my mind. I think readers of my notebook will benefit from a refresher."

Idyllica: "The exact thought I shared was this: 'together we may help individual seekers find PEACE OF MIND! Everyone who learns more about life, death, transformation and transcendence finds new vigor, happiness and joy for daily living, and feels great comfort and peace knowing what to expect when the limitations of the earth vibration are no longer in effect. *The Butterfly Revelation* INsights are the key, you know.'

"That was my affirmation. Now, you have carefully documented the unveiling of the *Revelation* scrawls as they were known by your caterpillar club friends. You have fulfilled your role to the utmost."

Casey: "Thank you."

Idyllica: "I sense that my embodiment with you is soon to end. You may be certain that I shall continue to enjoy a full-filled, eternal, state of being. As our time together has demonstrated to you, ***direct knowing*** is simply incomparable . . . and it is interminable!"

Casey: "Do you have a departing thought? Is there a final revelation? What do you have to say to the future readers of my notebook?"

Idyllica: "Woolly Bear expressed the simplest and most tranquil point-of-view that anyone can derive from *The Butterfly Revelation* point-of-viewing. Woolly Bear echoed a true and wise expression of the ancients as he waved goodbye to his creeping friends."

Casey: "I have a grand memory of Woolly's fond farewell."

Idyllica: "Yes, that was a telltale moment. Moving toward an unknowable future with only a vague understanding of what lay ahead, Woolly Bear revealed his utter peace-of-mind, a peace that one might say, 'passes beyond understanding.'

"Woolly's final words were 'I am at peace. I expect to live.' That is as fine a departing thought as one might have, is it not?"

Casey: "It was a beautiful moment. I believe that Woolly's great calm and confidence was, in no small part, directly attributable to *The Butterfly Revelation*. Is that also your departing thought?"

Idyllica: "I also have a heavenly revelation to offer you. In my present state, it is *continuously revealed to me* that I AM LOVED! ***Direct knowing*** this truth establishes an irrevocable bond with the creator, whose essence is LOVE."

Casey: "I interpret that to mean that you truly experience heaven on earth when you are with me. Is that accurate?"

Idyllica: "Indeed, though I am considered dead from an earth point-of-view, I have maintained my terrestrial vibration *potential*. I experience heaven, the LOVE of the Father, fully, boundlessly, interminably, wherever, whenever and however I choose to engage creation. Most importantly, I experience heaven *consciously*!"

Casey: "You have a heavenly state of being, or state-of-mind, I think I would say."

Idyllica: "Well understood, and my question to you as you think about living, cocooning, and dying, 'What is *your* present state of mind'?"

Casey: "Are you asking, 'what do I think and how do I feel about my own death?' Whoops, I mean my own 'transcendence'?"

Idyllica: "Yes. I am satisfied that you have been able to assimilate the wisdom of your human ancestors and the ancient INsights of *The Butterfly Revelation*. I think, concerning death, your readers now would be quite curious to know 'What is your own point-of-view?'"

Casey: "More than ever before, I accept with complete peace of mind and utmost confidence an assertion of the dying Master Teacher from Nazareth. He spoke to another man who was being crucified nearby. The man is reported to have asked the Master, Jesus, *to be remembered . . . when you come into your Kingdom.* The man was probably referring to The Kingdom *Of Heaven* about which the teacher had told many stories. Indeed, to those who had yearned for His teachings, the Galilean Rabbi had explained that this same 'Kingdom' was always *at hand . . .* for everyone!

"Jesus, responding to the request 'to be remembered,' replied with an *affirmation of transcendence* that would apply to them both upon their physical deaths. No conditions were mentioned. *Today, you shall be with me in Paradise.*

"That confident response, two millennia ago, from a dying man whose biography includes his having had the Holy Spirit descend upon him, to a dying man about whom nothing is known other than he was a lawbreaker, to me embodies the wisdom of *The Butterfly Revelation*."

Idyllica: "And do you resonate with that assurance?"

Casey: "Yes. 'In the twinkling of an eye . . . we shall put off our perishable nature and put on an imperishable nature,' is the language used in scriptures written in olden human times. You, yourself, capturing the INsights of *The Butterfly Revelation*, described a single moment of taking off your earth clothes (perishable) to enjoy unencumbered **direct knowing** (imperishable). To me, both are assurances describing our natural transcendence from terrestrial living to celestial living."

Idyllica: "I am happy to say that my time of indwelling with you in Spirit has come to a most refreshing end."

Casey: "I have been wondering about our future together especially since I am concerned that I haven't learned nearly as much from you as I'd like to know."

Idyllica: "You need not be concerned. Humans have a fond way of saying, 'I think you really get it.' Indeed, you do 'get it.' I **know** this to be true. After all, I **know** you!"

Casey: "Will I consciously unite with you ever again?"

Idyllica: "When you transcend, that is to say, when you achieve the destiny to which you were born, I remind you that 'you will know as you are known,' to quote your own spiritual heritage."

The spirit of the blue butterfly dazzler, has withdrawn. Will I enjoy an infusion of Idyllica's presence ever again? Is Idyllica real? Does Idyllica live? I only **know** what I experience. YES!

VIII
SURPRISE ENCOUNTER
Creating The Ultimate Scrawl

The final Caterpillar Club gathering did, indeed, occur on the day of Woolly Bear's early departure. I, however, returned to the same wisdom ring area for several days thereafter.

The very next day, there were a few caterpillars, but only two of the founders, the ever optimistic Melissa and the still lovely and adorable Pixie. As I tuned in to Pixie's vibration, I distinctly felt a sorrow that I believed would linger until Pixie herself had the urge to cocoon. She was expecting to see Monarchus IV, who did not appear. Sorely, she was experiencing the heartache of lost love.

One day, not even a week later, no caterpillars gathered, not even Pixie. My own heart was immediately sad, simply missing her, and The Caterpillar Club. I felt like an abandoned member-seeker.

Several days after that, as if a burst of sunlight flooded my entire being, I *knew* that Pixie was not at all dead, merely out of sight. Pixie had entered into her chrysalis state. Pixie was undergoing transformation. She was never again to be stuck in a creeper body. For Pixie, the chant she had led on that final day, the cocoon chant, was actually a picture of her future. I had a deep, tranquil sense that Pixie was about to exit the "gateway" which she herself had fashioned. Pixie would soon experience *flying*. I was filled with joy!

Do you remember how the Being & Becoming caterpillars defined "joy"? I went back to the earlier pages of this notebook to refresh my memory.

"JOY is basking in the light of a sunbeam," the caterpillars had agreed. As I now write, my entire being is filled with JOY as I bask in the sunshine of my memories of Pixie *knowing* that, after her current transformation, Pixie will continue to vibrate, albeit in a redesigned, *flying* body.

Pixie will continue to create new wavelengths. For all of creation this is good news. Any expansion involving Pixie's spirit will, undoubtedly, be full of the glue of LOVE, a love kindled during Pixie's time with The Caterpillar Club.

For Monarchus IV, I grieve as I do for my friends who die prematurely, that is, before enjoying their potential which remains unexplored. However, I am deeply satisfied that, in a way that was previously unthinkable to me, Monarchus IV lives. And, the love of Pixie that flickered fleetingly at the final Caterpillar Club gathering will be revealed to Monarchus IV as being a "plop" of pure LOVE, itself never dying.

Just a few weeks later, I must report a refreshing, new, *living* butterfly encounter. Following a definite yearning that I was feeling, I decided to revisit the site of The Caterpillar Club discussions. The experience was as remarkable and enlightening as was my first ever encounter with a living butterfly; remember, that was the day I met Monarchus III.

I found my former comfortable viewing spot. I saw no sign of creeper activity. I was about to fall asleep. My mind was drifting gently as my head was nodding. Suddenly, a bubbly, melodic, familiar "voice" tinkled clearly in my nearly empty mind. "Hi!" "How are you?" "You look happy." I knew that sound. PIXIE!?!

Casey: "Pixie! Is it truly you?"

Pixie: "I wondered if you would recognize me."

Casey: "I did not see you at first. Truly, I *knew* that you were somewhere nearby. You filled my mind and I *knew* your 'voice' as I used to experience it when, during your caterpillar time, you helped organize The Being & Becoming Bunch. The 'good old days' is the way we humans express enjoyable times past."

Pixie: "Oh, such memories. I treasure every one of them though I sometimes wonder what ever happened to Monarchus IV, a special, special companion to whom I never fully expressed my feelings when I had the opportunity. Even if he, too, experienced transformation, or flutteration, as I know it now, he might be unrecognizable to me. I don't know what he would look like *as a flyer*."

Casey: "I can confirm that he would look nothing like he did when he crept on the ground."

Pixie: "I look NOTHING like I did when I was a creeper! In fact, have you noticed, EVERYTHING about me is different?!?"

Casey: "Yes, I see you now. You are beautiful . . . and totally different. That is true."

Pixie: "Even so, you know who I am!"

Casey: "Yes. I have seen you *being* a caterpillar, and now I am seeing that you have *become* an astonishing, enchanting, sky-spanning butterfly. I loved you then, and I love you now. I am especially pleased that you now **know** the names which I gave you.

"In fact, Pixie, in a sense I cannot explain, I shared your affection for Monarchus IV. I, too, miss him. Yet, I am convinced that you and I both will meet Monarchus IV again."

Pixie: "Really? Where will that be?"

Casey: "It will not be a place *where we go*. Rather, it will be at a time *when we become* what humans call 'celestially' oriented. Now, you and I are 'terrestrially' oriented. There is no way for me to enable you to **know** what I mean. Trust that reunion with Monarchus IV is *possible*."

Pixie: "I am reminded of a *Butterfly Revelation* fragment that I could not grasp as a caterpillar. *Trust The Cocoon . . . gateway to the sky*. At the time, I did not **know** how to trust the point-of-view which the INsight contained. Now that I have experienced the cocoon, and I fly freely in the sky, I fully appreciate the message for the truth it contained. Needless to say, I have a different point-of-viewing."

Casey: "To look back and appreciate is satisfying. More difficult, is to look ahead and have nothing but trust upon which to rely."

Pixie: "I trust *you*."

Casey: "That is an honor especially as my point-of-viewing is different from yours. Granting that, I invite you to open your mind to the *possibility* of a grand reunion with the spirit of Monarchus IV."

Pixie: "I embrace the *possibility* though it is unclear what you mean by the spirit of my beloved Monarchus IV."

Casey: "Though the idea may seem foggy to you, I promise that, in spirit, you will one day **know** Monarchus IV and **be known** by him. When you no longer can fly, you will discard your wings taking on a new spirit way of being as amazingly different as your flying world is different from your former caterpillar world. Trust me."

Pixie: "Your promise stirs my heart and calms my mind. I am experiencing a comforting peace-of-mind. In the past, thinking about someone who had disappeared, whether alive or dead, resulted in my feeling unexplainable remorse.

"Now, with the assurance of reunion with my long lost Monarchus IV in mind, I am experiencing a peace that is beyond my understanding. I never expected to feel this way as long as I lived. Is it because I trust your message even though I cannot fully grasp its truth?"

Casey: "Perhaps. I am not certain. You are the first I **know** to experience a special peace-of-mind that to me was foretold.

"I was assured peace-of-mind would happen if I were to reveal what I was learning from *The Butterfly Revelation*. I absorbed the promise while sharing celestial moments with an ancient butterfly spirit. Today, your 'peace bath,' as I am going to call it, has strengthened my resolve to trust that LOVING spirit, whom I *know* as Idyllica."

Pixie: "Well, if I were you, I would absolutely trust the source of the peace-of-mind prophecy you see being fulfilled in me today. Now that I have come through the cocoon gateway, I realize *The Butterfly Revelation* itself is a source of much more than speculation. The *Revelation* is infused with truth and transformative ways of thinking from those who have lived and, indeed, actualized the INsights. As a seeker, I merely meditated on the perplexing destiny promise, *You Were Born To Fly*. Now, I, too, am living it."

Casey: "What else are you experiencing as a flyer that has changed the perspective you had as a creeper? I'd like to include that in my special notebook, if I may."

Pixie: "Be my guest. Ha, that was a retort that Woolly Bear used to give when someone asked, 'Is it O.K.?'

"I miss Woolly, too. There was a time when he became so enamored of his own quips that I nicknamed him, 'Woolly The Puff.' I was so happy when he dropped the attitude and really dug into the *Revelation* scrawls with the rest of us. I smile when I think of Woolly. Do you know if he and Monarchus IV also became butterflyers?"

Casey: "Monarchus IV actually omitted the transformation-to-butterfly moment in his life."

Pixie: "Omitted? You mean he skipped this wondrous sky life? What in the world does that mean?"

Casey: "What Monarchus IV did, we humans call 'transcendence.' The explanation would be as incomprehensible to you now as flying was unfathomable to you as a caterpillar. Nevertheless, I can assure you that for Monarchus IV the change was utterly marvelous, though the moment of its happening wasn't nearly as intriguing as the *way of transformation* that involves cocooning."

Pixie: "Was anyone else present when Monarchus IV, My Dear, experienced this transcendence?"

Casey: "Yes, as a matter of fact there was someone present, someone you deftly avoided during your caterpillar days. The one witness to Monarchus's transcendence was Sir Charles Mantis, whom the Mantis clan calls, 'Charlie.' Other insects call him 'Chucklin' Charlie.' I was not there, but I learned that Sir Charles was chuckling when Monarchus IV was last seen."

Pixie: "Sounds like an extraordinary occasion. I must say that I am glad I wasn't there. The entire Mantis clan always leered at me whenever I was near any one of them."

Casey: "You fortunately avoided this preying clan. I learned that they live only for themselves and only for today, quite unlike your family. And, they *are* dangerous."

Pixie: "Yes, our family always looked ahead holding on to a foggy dream. With Monarchus IV and Wooly Bear, the dream was that *we are born to fly.* It was incomprehensible, but it turned out to be true. How you look at things makes all the difference in how you act.

"When Monarchus IV announced that he would no longer study the *Revelation* scrawls, my heart skipped several beats. When he changed his mind, my energy soared. So, how you look at life affects others as well as yourself, believe me!"

Casey: "Again, if I may be your guest and make a note or two, tell me if you have any new ways of looking at things, any different perspectives, now that you are flyer."

Pixie: "Well, we butterflies sing as we gather. We call it 'yodeling.' The ritual is a holdover from our days as caterpillar seekers.

Casey: "Are the words to your song the same as those you chanted when you met with Woolly, Monarchus IV, and the others during your caterpillar days?"

Pixie: "Unlike the caterpillar chant, our butterfly ritual yodel is not a transformation Destiny Chant nor a Destiny Yodel. No butterfly, so far as we know, has ever reappeared in any form after he or she stops drinking, dries out and withers away.

"That is to say, in the absence of water in its body, no butterfly has ever been seen to be alive. We yodel, therefore, based not so much upon our experience, but much more upon our hope and, even more, upon our faith."

Casey: "I am fascinated. Tell me more about this 'hope' and 'faith' of which you speak?"

Pixie: "There is a bit of explaining that I need to do first." During my caterpillar life, I experienced a connection with Monarchus IV that seemed deeper, more intense, than the feeling of just being close, snuggling, adoring. Even when he was not in my presence, I felt an amazing connection, the word for which I was told, is 'love.'

"I do not know much more about the meaning of the word, but others have told me that they have had similar moments. These are fleeting moments when you report that someone else was present more completely than just in your memory. It could mean that 'love' doesn't die out due to absence or distance. Does this make sense?"

Casey: "Yes. One expression humans use is, 'present in spirit.' *Remembering* is one thing. A real *sense of someone else's presence* is another matter altogether. Interestingly, I have recently had this *sense experience* with a long deceased butterfly spirit. The sensation was nearly identical to what you described. The only phrase that seemed appropriate then and seems authentic now, is 'love connection.'

"I felt enveloped and permeated by a real substance that I could only imagine was some portion of an absolutely universal ingredient of all life. I label that amazing ingredient LOVE. According to ancient human wisdom, it is the glue of creation."

172

Pixie: "Interestingly, our butterfly hope is similar to the 'love connection' you imagine being an ingredient of all life. Our hope, too, includes the conviction that something of ourselves is universal in substance and duration. I suppose you could say 'hope yodeling' describes our ritual."

Casey: "I take it that *you* do not use 'hope yodeling' to describe your in-gathering routine. I would like to learn how you and your flying friends do explain the ritual singing. You apparently do not use 'hope' to define your primary motivation for gathering and for yodeling. I am overwhelmingly curious to learn more about your current transformed perspective."

Pixie: "You are correct. We do not use the word 'hope' because hope is not something we actually experience. Hope implies that we have no assurance about a future situation. Some would say 'wishful thinking' is a better way of describing what individuals do who are 'hoping' something will be true. We butterflies, on the other hand, have an unshakable belief that our song contains the absolute truth concerning our final destiny, our life beyond sky flying."

Casey: "Please, share your conviction."

———

Not surprisingly, at this moment, I am experiencing a seemingly unquenchable curiosity about Pixie and her butterflying friends.

Coincidently, I initially met Pixie because Monarchus IV's father had urged that, if I were ever to experience 'unquenchable curiosity' about the *The Butterfly Revelation*, I ought to find Monarchus IV and the caterpillar seekers. Of course, as you know, I did find them.

Admittedly, I do have unquenchable curiosity. As a matter of fact, if I were asked for one key to finding new truths about life, death, and life hereafter, I would say it is unquenchable curiosity."

––––

Pixie: "We call our choral ritual a 'Love Lullaby.' The lullaby includes what we **know**. We also embrace and we sing tenderly what we are **yet to know**. Here, let me yodel for you."

I love, you love, we love.
After Terra Time
We shall love...
And BE LOVED.

The sound was similar to delicate wind chimes tinkling. I have heard handbells played with a similar charming plinking.

Casey: "Am I correct to understand that after Terra Time means 'after your life on earth'?"

Pixie: "Yes, and there is an intoxicating truth in our gathering melody that applies both to our Terra Time life and our ATT life. As you listened to the lullaby, did you pick up on the one aspect of Terra Time life that does not pass away?"

Casey: "If you mean 'love,' I heard it loudly and clearly. In your lullaby, love is located both in the present and in the future. Is this a special sort of truth for butterflies?"

Pixie: "Indeed, it is. I, personally, *know* the truth about love being vital in both my past and my present. Some day I shall *know* the love that will be vitally alive in my future. After I embed my eggs for the next generation, I will create a scrawl that will offer this truth in an abbreviated form. My desire will be to find a cooperative snail who can smear it openly for my caterpillar offspring to ponder."

Casey: "Oh yes, please! Please do explain what you believe to be the truth about love. It would be my great good fortune to receive a butterfly INsight even before it is written, and it would also be priceless for my human readers. You would do me great honor to reveal to me a future *Revelation* 'beacon' before it is scrawled."

Pixie: "Very well."

There is a notable pause indicating the next ideas are of paramount importance. I have never experienced greater curiosity.

Pixie: "Human-whom-I love, you live because you have *water*. You love because you have *soul*. When you no longer have a water life, your Terra Life, your soul will live *because you will continue to be LOVED*. You will leave behind your need for water."

Casey: "In earth terms, I will be dead. You said, 'dried out, withered.' 'Dust to dust,' we say."

Pixie: "Ahhhh. Not so. You simply break free from your dependence upon water. You escape your earth shell. *You will never get beyond the LOVE in which every cell of your body has been bathed from the very first moment of your birth*. No one can get beyond or outside LOVE. That is our conviction. We butterflyers have a word for this all pervading marvel: FLUTTER!"

Casey: "I have learned this. And, you have thought of your own INsight scrawl which captures and communicates the butterflying conviction about which you yodel?"

Pixie: (triumphantly) *"LOVE Endures Forever."*

Casey: "Suppose I want to know how to test such a conviction. Suppose I want evidence. Suppose I want to be certain. I want to be enLIGHTened. I want something I can believe with all my heart!"

Pixie: "To me, in my caterpillar time, I had the same desire. I was certain that I was missing something that I could somehow find outside myself. I helped start The Being & Becoming Bunch because I thought, by striving together, seekers would find the secret missing ingredient."

Casey: "What have you found? What is the truth? What DO you believe?"

Pixie: "The great love secret, truly an incomparable INsight, has been within my being all along. I simply did not unveil it. I was born of a butterfly egg, not a caterpillar egg. I was *Born To Fly*, as the *Revelation* declared. I now realize, *I Was Born To Love*, too. Though we never found an ancient scrawl which affirmed it, I *know* we are all FLUTTER! born."

Casey: "And what do you think is the secret I am not finding?"

Pixie: "You, too, have already been impregnated with the very light you seek. You **know** the secret. You have experienced the truth. You need no longer look outside yourself."

Casey: "Light? Secret? Truth? Please, give me words to believe."

Pixie: "Odd. I am experiencing a loving presence who seems, in some way, like a magnificent blue butterfly I once saw during my caterpillar days. The visitor is answering your desire for words to believe. The message is the visitor's, yet I feel it is mine as well. We seem united in the moment."

I recognize the vibration. Idyllica is here! Idyllica is communicating . . . through Pixie! As before, I clearly understand.

"You were born of spirit, of LOVE, embedded in each living cell of your being.

You were not born of human egg and spermatozoon alone.

You, Casey, were born to *transcend* earth."

Casey: "Born of spirit . . . a blinding truth!"

At this point, there occurred a quiet spell of undetermined length. Pixie is dreamily flying farther and farther away.

Casey: "Pixie, wait! Please, do you yourself have any words of advice for the here and now?"

Pixie: [fading] "I continue to feel a presence which identifies itself as 'Idyllica.' The answer to your advice question seems to be coming directly through me for you."

I am thoroughly filled with the now-familiar spirit of the dazzling blue butterfly, Idyllica! I am receiving words-without-words. As usual, I understand them.

Idyllica: (An incomparable blended "voice" incorporating the magical tones of Pixie and the majestic resonance of indelible spirit)

**"For the rest of your terrestrial sojourn,
I offer these words to live by:**

**1) Above all, and in all, seek LOVE
(The 'Kingdom Of God')**
which is always at hand.

**2) Be devoted to LOVE
(Your 'Creator')**
*with all your heart,
mind, strength and soul.*

**3) Give LOVE to all mankind
(Share 'The Holy Spirit')**
*as if each individual were,
in fact, your very own self."*

Pixie: "Does this advice make sense to you? Is it all new to you?"

Casey: "Oh no, it is not new. This is very old advice which continues to hide in plain sight just as *The Butterfly Revelation* beacons are often hidden in plain sight. I simply had pretty much skimmed over the deeper meaning. I had not been as diligent a seeker as you and Monarchus IV and Woolly Bear."

Pixie: [farther away] "Oh, there is a bit more. The visitor is speaking again."

—⁓—

Congruously, I am so in sync with this spirit source that I am beginning to think that the thoughts are my very own. The INsights no longer seem to belong to someone else who is simply sharing them with me. Though it is my name I hear, I am certain that the point-of-view is part of a universal *knowing* and is available to everyone.

—⁓—

Idyllica: (With uncommon emphasis) **"Casey, it is your heritage to experience the Kingdom Of Heaven *now*, as well as for all eternity. You were born into the great creation of LOVE. LOVE is your rightful inheritance, bequeathed from the Creator-Of-All.**

"Whether you live in your terrestrial body, or cocoon and emerge in your celestial glory, remember: The Kingdom Of Heaven, the transcendent vibration of LOVE, is always *at hand*. Within this grand kingdom, you live, you move, you have your being . . . NOW and interminably!"

Pixie: (wispy) "Idyllica, who is addressing you now as 'partner,' has one final thought."

I hear a voice which must be 'heavenly' in origin and expression. To me, the sound carries a vibratory blend beyond any sound I have ever heard. My entire being is tingling. I am immersed. I know why individuals throughout history have exclaimed, "I heard the voice of God!" That is the sensation I am experiencing. I am being overwhelmingly LOVED!

The final thought is not unexpected. It has been reported that shepherds heard a heavenly chorus sing the same thought when announcing the birth of a special child two millennia ago.

"PEACE ON EARTH . . . as it is in heaven!"

I am somewhat amazed at the depth of my conversation with *butterfly* Pixie. And now she is winging translucently away. Even in the exquisite way she barely dances upon the flowers on which she descends, Pixie has a lightness of style.

My friends would say, "She's something else!" Someday, I would like to hear Pixie and her friends yodeling together.

Who could know that, after encountering the insect world of my mother's garden, my own mind would begin to experience the great peace that I am now enjoying? My question now is how to share the peace with others.

What's this? Once more, I sense Idyllica. I empty my thoughts. Oh my! A swoosh of LOVE! I have the certainty that Idyllica has remained to offer encouragement and a final word *in complete harmony* with me.

Idyllica: "Casey, you and I are peace-partners in spirit. Now, you must use your special gift of revealing."

The voice drops to an intimate whisper as belonging to a trusted mentor leaning over to offer the most confidential thought.

Idyllica: "Finish the Bug Book. For anyone who has ever asked, 'What is to become of me when I die?' your notebook contains a priceless treasure. *The Butterfly Revelation*, nurturing peace-of-mind, is that treasure. Though priceless, *The Butterfly Revelation* is free. It is a gift of LOVE! "

With that challenge, "finish the Bug Book," Idyllica has withdrawn. The whisper is gone.

Suddenly, I have a consuming thought, "I *shall* finish the Bug Book!" The impression is clearly more than a handful of words. I am *experiencing* this thought without words, an overflowing moment of Idyllic Inspiration. What I am feeling is an irrepressible urge. "I shall finish! I promise!"

———

I have been blessed to experience the transcended spirit of a long absent butterfly. Through our interwoven minds, I have glimpsed heaven while remaining terra firmly alive on the earth.

This yoked spirit happening is resulting in an infusion of peace of mind, a kind of inoculation against any anxiety about dying. Indeed, I have developed a new point-of-viewing.

Frequently, I find myself reflecting upon the clash between the Mantis Family view of life and the Monarch Family way of life. It is as though "war" meets "peace" and "war" wins the day.

My new point-of-viewing, originating during my merges with Idyllica, causes me to conclude that war only wins on earth because, throughout mankind, the terrestrial vibes dominate. If celestial vibes were to dominate, peace would win.

That outcome, of course, would require men and women everywhere on earth to "seek ye first the Kingdom Of God," according to the Galilean rabbi. He was suggesting that we humans find heaven, the celestial LOVE vibe, deep within, and live out its influence. His prayer, "thy kingdom come on earth as it is in heaven," would be fulfilled. Peace would then win the day . . . every day!

Consequently, I have concluded that it really is *possible* to experience heaven on earth. To say such a state is *impossible* will, as Idyllica suggested, shut down the human mind, closing out the most creative ways that we, amazing plops of consciousness, might create overwhelming LOVE where discord and limitation now prevail. After all, with our minds we are creating creation every moment of every day.

Upon my becoming free from the terrestrial body in which I now live, I am certain I will enjoy utterly the beauty of everything. My transcendence may happen an hour from now, a week from now, or five decades from now. That no longer is of any consequence to me. I know what the future holds and what eternity holds. Both are simply the moments of "now" which are yet to come.

I shall not expect to go to some far different place to experience heaven. I shall expect to become different, to move out of my 'terrestrial tent' into a 'celestial mansion,' with which to experience life everlasting in a way unfathomable to a tent dweller.

I am at peace. I expect to live . . . interminably.

IX
GOODBYE CASEY CRAWLEY
unquenchably curious - contented

Casey Crawley's corpse lay innocently in a satin lined coffin at the front of the small chapel. Every visitor, most of whom were friends of the widow, Cassandra Crawley, made an almost identical remark before leaving the chapel. "I have never seen anyone look so peaceful . . . even happy." They apparently had not picked up on a particular detail in the newspaper story, a detail that was reported by the first rescuer at the accident scene.

Several hours after the horrific landslide had swept Casey's car off the road down into a precipitous ravine, a jaws-of-life machine was finally able to reach the crushed car. The first report from the scene contained an off-hand remark.

"I was dumbfounded that the car was not crushed flat. It looked more like a cocoon. When we broke in to free the driver, we realized that he had died only moments before. He had been encased in that protective shell for many hours. Though he must have known he had no way out, he showed no sign of desperation such as a panicky grimace permanently frozen on his face. Quite the contrary, I have never seen a lifeless victim who looked so contented. There was even a smile on his face."

On a table in the chapel foyer, Casey's mother had arranged three items. On the right side was an open guest register with a liquid gel pen beside it. Each one who signed would later receive a special butterfly brooch, or pendant, from the large collection that Casey had acquired. The other items on the table were somewhat unusual for an ordinary funeral environment.

Beside the register, in a new flower pot, was a milkweed plant, a somewhat odd floral piece for the occasion, wouldn't you say? Casey's mother, who never doubted her little bug boy, said simply, "Casey believed it drew 'orange flutterers' to linger nearby." Her friends were bemused and assured each other that, to be honest, the widow Crawley, too, had always been a little different.

The third item was a well-worn, heavy notebook, partially open, standing on its end so that portions of several loose leaf pages could be seen. The odd notebook might not have attracted much attention had it not been for the extravagantly colored cover.

Vivid splashes of indescribable beauty completely blanketed the notebook's cover. The colors were magnetic, compelling, absorbing. Every person approaching the guest register stopped cold and stared, spellbound, at the notebook.

Upon closer examination, the magic of the cover was disclosed. Each "color splash" was formed by a single, hand drawn butterfly wing! Casey had carefully reproduced and mingled the exacting uniqueness of countless species. "Utterly amazing," said several guests. Others were simply speechless, awestricken, upon realizing how Casey had created the cover.

Subtly, by means of *The Butterfly Revelation* notebook cover alone, Casey's incomparable gift of revealing touches the mind and heart as God, artist hands, butterfly wings and an observer become ONE. Indeed, the glorious wings themselves reveal an eternal INsight: The loving, healing, indescribable Creator-Of-All is always *at hand*.

You may remember, it was Monarchus III, the first butterfly with whom Casey connected, who had prophesied this moment. Casey recorded that the bright orange flippity-flopper had said, "Ah, 'Kay-SEE,' a name that you should cherish. You have INsight, which is the ability to 'see' within another. It is an extraordinary characteristic, somewhat rare, I might add. I predict that you will become a very special 'see-er,' one who can reveal INsights drawn from our insect world to curious individuals in your human world."

The notebook that Casey's mother so lovingly placed on the chapel table seemed almost alive, indeed, to FLUTTER! One fascinated friend said, "I think that book could fly on its own."

Inside, the pages were filled with Casey's descriptions of interactions he had had with many kinds of living creatures from the time he was four years old. The notebook was the Bug Boy's private memoir, his 'Bug Book.' As foretold, it was truly a see-er's revelation.

The notebook contained much more than *descriptions* of Casey's encounters with bugs and insects in his yard. The notebook included *conversations*!

One significant section was an actual *transcription* of Casey's resonating involvement with a butterfly, MONARCHUS III. Such an occurrence was previously unknown among humans.

It is important to note, even for Cassy Crawley's dearest friends, the "butterfly thing" was just too preposterous. Among themselves, the widow's friends agreed that Casey had made the whole thing up. Privately they scoffed at the idea of an actual Caterpillar Club.

Notwithstanding doubters, because of his immense curiosity, determination, and love for bugs and insects, Casey indeed was led to a group of wisdom seeking caterpillars and was introduced to *The Butterfly Revelation*. In his notebook, Casey wrote details of daily encounters with the so-called Caterpillar Club, the moniker he gave to gatherings of his insect friends.

The Butterfly Revelation contained INsights from transformed caterpillars (i.e., butterflies!) discerned at a time in the ancient past, a time that no living caterpillar could determine precisely. Casey learned that in each generation there were curious, persistent and, occasionally, love-driven caterpillars who rediscovered *The Revelation*.

The caterpillar seekers with whom Casey interacted were studying recently discovered *Revelation* fragments. Several readable scrawls had been found smeared on leaves drooping over a nearby path. These transformative INsights were faithfully recorded in Casey's notebook.

Casey also transcribed the deeper meanings that entered his consciousness through a butterfly "spirit," a living mind that had transcended both its caterpillar and its butterfly nature. Utterly unprecedented! The butterfly spirit described the INsights as beacons bringing light to anyone who wonders about the "shadow of death" experience that all living beings anticipate.

What Casey included in his special notebook is no more and no less than a point-of-viewing obtained from a source different from any that had previously been discovered by humans. The entries are first vibration accounts of the activities of a group of backyard crawlers that Casey dubbed The Caterpillar Club. Casey's notebook, which he titled, *The Butterfly Revelation*, revealed a universal wisdom, wisdom for living, loving, and dying. In a word, priceless!

Casey Crawley's special notebook was last seen at the graveyard. The widow, Cassandra "Cassy" Crawley, intended to throw the legacy Bug Book into her son's grave. She was finally alone after her friends and a small group of mourners had departed. A grave digger standing nearby later mentioned to a colleague what he had seen.

"This lady started to toss a big book on to the casket into the hole we dug, but she couldn't seem to let go. Finally, she just walked away with the book under her arm."

THE END

This notebook dedicated with LOVE
to the memory of the founders*
and first gatherers of

The Caterpillar Club

*"Pixie" Melanis
"Vanessa" Cardui
"Melissa" Lycaeides
*"Woolly Bear" Arctiidae
"Janice" Janais Chlosyne
"Buckeye, Jr." Junonia Coenia
*"Monarchus" Danais Plexippus
"Emperor Lawrence" Doxocopa Laurentia

"Woolly Bear" Arctiidae
"Woolly is a splendid caterpillar
both in appearance and demeanor."

"Monarchus" Plexippus
"was disenchanted with the
munch-and-meander
way of life into
which he had
been born"

189

A Unique Point-Of-Viewing

Bettye & Ed Frierson

Bettye and I are the biological parents of six children, including TWO SETS OF TWINS! Honestly, we are now ex-Ringmasters, mostly spectators, of the "Frierson Family Circus" which includes 22 grandchildren, a handful of next generation in-laws, and four "greats." We've been at this *together* about 60 years!

More than 20 years ago, I told the following anecdote to begin the memorial service honoring our eldest daughter, Suzan, who had died in an automobile accident. Our newest infant granddaughter was present and we were seeing her for the first time.

> Holding up a well worn ax, the farmer exclaimed, "We have had this same ax in our family for more than three generations. It has had three different heads and four different handles!"

Though the accident occurred more than 20 years ago, we do miss our Suzan daily. Joyously, that infant granddaughter was married this year! Indeed, we have had the same "spirit" in our family for three PLUS generations. We daily experience that same "spirit" emanating from both the here and the hereafter.

I have written this story to explain what I have learned about the existence of our "spirit nature" and to share my answer to the question, "What happens when you die?"

"Dr. Ed" Frierson

FLUTTER! Wisdom For Living, Loving, Dying

Published By The BOOKCOMBER

- For Those Seeking Treasure In Books -

Paperback Edition: [amazon.com]
E-Book Edition: [kindle.com]
Audio Edition: [audible.com]

www.ingramcontent.com/pod-product-compliance
Lightning Source LLC
LaVergne TN
LVHW011229080426
835509LV00005B/395